VOICES

HEARING GOD
IN A WORLD OF
IMPOSTORS

Old Testament

by

pam gillaspie

**Voices: Hearing God in a World of
Impostors, Old Testament**

Copyright © 2025 by Pam Gillaspie
Published by Ignite Bible Ministires
www.pamgillaspie.com

ISBN 978-1-960938-11-4

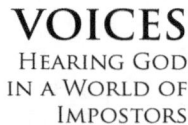

VOICES
HEARING GOD
IN A WORLD OF
IMPOSTORS

Old Testament

Dedicated to . . .

Jan Silvious, of all the wisdom you've passed my way over the years, nothing
surpasses your bottom-line query . . . *Where is it written?* Thank you for always
pointing to the plumb line and for tirelessly helping me apply truth with wisdom.

Kay Arthur, thank you for always standing doggedly for truth in the midst of a
crooked and perverse generation. It is my honor to partner with you for the further-
ance of the Gospel of Jesus Christ.

VOICES
Hearing God in a World of Impostors

Old Testament

There is nothing quite like your favorite pair of jeans. You can dress them up, you can dress them down. You can work in them, play in them, shop in them . . . live in them. They always feel right. It is my hope that the structure of this Bible study will fit you like those jeans; that it will work with your life right now, right where you are whether you're new to this whole Bible thing or whether you've been studying the Book for years!

How is this even possible? Smoke and mirrors, perhaps? The new mercilessly thrown in the deep end? The experienced given pompoms and the job of simply cheering others on? None of the above.

Flexible inductive Bible studies are designed with options that will allow you to go as deep each week as you desire. If you're just starting out and feeling a little overwhelmed, stick with the main text and don't think a second thought about the sidebar assignments. If you're looking for a challenge, then take the sidebar prompts and go ahead and dig all the way to China! As you move along through the study, think of the sidebars and "Digging Deeper" boxes as that 2% of lycra that you find in certain jeans . . . the wiggle-room that will help them fit just right.

Beginners may find that they want to start adding in some of the optional assignments as they go along. Experts may find that when three children are throwing up for three days straight, foregoing those assignments for the week is the way to live wisely.

Life has a way of ebbing and flowing and this study is designed to ebb and flow right along with it!

ENJOY!

Contents

VOICES
Hearing God in a World of Impostors

Old Testament

HOW TO USE THIS STUDY

Flexible inductive Bible studies meet you where you are and take you as far as you want to go.

1. WEEKLY STUDY: The main text guides you through the complete topic of study for the week.

2. FYI boxes: For Your Information boxes provide bite-sized material to shed additional light on the topic.

3. ONE STEP FURTHER and other sidebar boxes: Sidebar boxes give you the option to push yourself a little further. If you have extra time or are looking for an extra challenge, you can try one, all, or any number in between! These boxes give you the ultimate in flexibility.

4. DIGGING DEEPER boxes: If you're looking to go further, Digging Deeper sections will help you sharpen your skills as you continue to mine the truths of Scripture for yourself.

> ## FYI:
> **Reading Tip: Begin with Prayer**
> You may have heard this a million times over and if this is a million and one, so be it. Whenever you read or study God's Word, first pray and ask His Spirit to be your Guide.

> ## ONE STEP FURTHER:
> **Word Study: *torah*/law**
> The first of eight Hebrew key words we encounter for God's Word is *torah* translated "law." If you're up for a challenge this week, do a word study to learn what you can about *torah*. Run a concordance search and examine where the word *torah* appears in the Old Testament and see what you can learn from the contexts.
>
> If you decide to look for the word for "law" in the New Testament, you'll find that the primary Greek word is *nomos*.
>
> Be sure to see what Paul says about the law in Galatians 3 and what Jesus says in Matthew 5.

> ## Digging Deeper
> **What else does God's Word say about counselors?**
> If you can, spend some time this week digging around for what God's Word says about counselors.
>
> Start by considering what you already know about counsel from the Word of God and see if you can actually show where these truths are in the Bible. Make sure that the Word actually says what you think it says.

WEEK ONE
What Voices are Calling?

My sheep hear My voice,
and I know them, and they follow Me . . .

—*Jesus,* John 10:27

Jesus warned His disciples that in times to come "false Christs and false prophets will arise and will show great signs and wonders, so as to mislead, if possible, even the elect" (Matthew 24:24). In a world of sensational spiritual claims, do you ever wonder when you should listen and when you should run? It's time to stop wondering and start discovering biblical answers. Examining the Bible for ourselves, we'll look at how God has communicated with people over the ages, as well as at the biblical accounts of other voices that seek to destroy so we can learn to discern and stand firm in these last days. While *Voices Part One* focuses on the Old Testament, we'll start with an overview of the nature of Scripture as we begin.

FYI:

If You're in a Class
Complete **Week One** together on your first day of class. This will be a great way to start getting to know one another and will help those who are newer to Bible study get their bearings.

VOICES
HEARING GOD
IN A WORLD OF
IMPOSTORS

Old Testament

CONSIDER the WAY you THINK

As we start our study, we need to examine our presuppositions and define terms. For now, let's consider what views we're bringing to the table.

How do you think God speaks today?

Why do you believe this?

If someone said "God told me to . . .", how would you respond?

What is your view of Scripture's authority? How much "say" should it have in your life?

What about Scripture's sufficiency? Is it "enough" to answer life's questions?

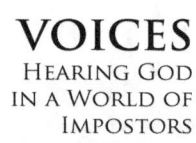

Digging Deeper

Read or Listen through Genesis

While the workbook will include specific instances of God speaking, the best way to identify these occurrences is to read the Book for yourself. If you're up for it this week, read or listen through Genesis to identify times when God speaks to people and times when contrary, deceptive voices counter His truth. Jot down your notes below so you can compare what you've identified with what we'll be studying together.

God Speaks

Others Speak

Summary

FYI:

Start with Prayer
You've probably heard it before and if we study together in the future, you're sure to hear it again. Whenever you read or study God's Word, first pray and ask His Spirit to be your Guide. Jesus says that the Spirit will lead us into all truth.

FOUNDATIONS

Before we start systematically working our way through the Bible, let's see what the Bible says about itself.

SETTING the SCENE

Anticipating his imminent death, Paul writes Timothy, his son in the faith, telling him what he needs to know about life and ministry.

OBSERVE the TEXT of SCRIPTURE

READ 2 Timothy 3:14-17. **MARK** every reference to *Scripture*, including synonyms. **UNDERLINE** everything Paul says the Scriptures can do.

2 Timothy 3:14-17

14 *You, however, continue in the things you have learned and become convinced of, knowing from whom you have learned them,*

15 *and that from childhood you have known the sacred writings which are able to give you the wisdom that leads to salvation through faith which is in Christ Jesus.*

16 *All Scripture is inspired by God and profitable for teaching, for reproof, for correction, for training in righteousness;*

17 *so that the man of God may be adequate, equipped for every good work.*

DISCUSS with your GROUP or PONDER on your own . . .

What does Paul instruct Timothy to do in verse 14?

What had Timothy already done that enabled him to follow Paul's instruction?

FYI:

Inspired by God

The Greek word translated "inspired by God" is *theopneustos* and literally means "God breathed" or "God spirited." It appears only in the New Testament in 2 Timothy 3:16.

VOICES
HEARING GOD
IN A WORLD OF
IMPOSTORS

Old Testament

What sacred writings does Paul refer to? What were they able to do?

What does Paul say about the nature of Scripture? What does it do? Why is this important?

At the point of his writing, what scriptures would Timothy have known from his childhood? Explain.

SETTING the SCENE

The apostle Peter, an eye-witness to the life and ministry of Jesus, comments on Paul's letters.

OBSERVE the TEXT of SCRIPTURE

READ 2 Peter 3:14-18 and **MARK** every reference to *Paul*, including pronouns.
UNDERLINE every reference to those who distort Scripture and/or promote error.

2 Peter 3:14-18

14 *Therefore, beloved, since you look for these things, be diligent to be found by Him in peace, spotless and blameless,*

15 *and regard the patience of our Lord as salvation; just as also our beloved brother Paul, according to the wisdom given him, wrote to you,*

ONE STEP
FURTHER:

Read 2 Timothy
If you have time this week, go ahead and read through Paul's complete letter to Timothy. It's only four chapters long. Record your observations below.

VOICES
HEARING GOD
IN A WORLD OF
IMPOSTORS

Old Testament

16 as also in all his letters, speaking in them of these things, in which are some things hard to understand, which the untaught and unstable distort, as they do also the rest of the Scriptures, to their own destruction.

17 You therefore, beloved, knowing this beforehand, be on your guard so that you are not carried away by the error of unprincipled men and fall from your own steadfastness,

18 but grow in the grace and knowledge of our Lord and Savior Jesus Christ. To Him be the glory, both now and to the day of eternity. Amen.

FYI:

Peter's View of Paul

While Peter was an eye-witness to Jesus' life and ministry, Paul was converted after Jesus rose from the dead, ascended into heaven, and appeared to him. Before this Paul hunted and persecuted Christians. Peter, writing under the inspiration of the Holy Spirit, attested to Paul's inspiration also.

ONE STEP FURTHER:

Word Study: Scriptures

If you have some extra time this week, find the Greek word for "Scriptures." Then check out how else it is used in the rest of the New Testament. Record your findings below.

DISCUSS with your GROUP or PONDER on your own . . .

How does Peter describe Paul?

How does he describe Paul's writings? What does this imply? Explain.

Besides Paul, who else does Peter talk about? What characterizes these people? What do they do? What will be their end?

Why are they dangerous to Peter's readers?

How can you identify and stand in the face of similar threats today?

VOICES
HEARING GOD
IN A WORLD OF
IMPOSTORS

Old Testament

Digging Deeper

Jesus and the Scriptures

Peter and Paul had views on the nature of Scripture, and so did Jesus! If you have time this week, examine the Gospels to see what Jesus said about the Scriptures and record your findings below. A simple way to start is to use a concordance (via book, software, or website) to search on the term "Scripture." Of course you'll never be disappointed by reading the full accounts so you won't miss synonyms and allusions to the Old Testament.

Matthew

Mark

Luke

John

Summary:

ONE STEP FURTHER:

Word Study: Destruction
What does Peter mean when he talks about "destruction" in 2 Peter 3:16? If you have time this week, find the Greek word and see how it's used elsewhere in the New Testament. Record your findings below.

OBSERVE the TEXT of SCRIPTURE

READ Hebrews 1:1-2 and **MARK** the word *spoke/spoken*.

Hebrews 1:1-2

1 God, after He spoke long ago to the fathers in the prophets in many portions and in many ways,

2 in these last days has spoken to us in His Son, whom He appointed heir of all things, through whom also He made the world.

DISCUSS with your GROUP or PONDER on your own . . .

How did God speak long ago? Who did He speak to?

How has He spoken in these last days?

Should we expect God to speak "in many portions and in many ways" now? Explain your answer.

BACK TO THE BEGINNING

We've seen this week that all Scripture is God-breathed. It is all the revelation of God to His people. As we proceed in our study, let's keep this truth in the forefront of our minds.

ONE STEP FURTHER:

Watch the Verb Tenses

What verb tense does the author of Hebrews use for "spoke" and "has spoken"? What is significant about it? Why does it matter? Record your findings below.

ONE STEP FURTHER:

Long Ago and Last Days

If you have some extra time this week, examine the phrases "long ago" and "in these last days." What time frames is the author talking about in relation to where we are in history? Record your findings below.

VOICES
HEARING GOD
IN A WORLD OF
IMPOSTORS

Old Testament

OBSERVE the TEXT of SCRIPTURE

READ Genesis 1–3 for an overview; then **READ** Genesis 1 and **MARK** the verb *said*.

Genesis 1

1 In the beginning God created the heavens and the earth.

2 The earth was formless and void, and darkness was over the surface of the deep, and the Spirit of God was moving over the surface of the waters.

3 Then God said, "Let there be light"; and there was light.

4 God saw that the light was good; and God separated the light from the darkness.

5 God called the light day, and the darkness He called night. And there was evening and there was morning, one day.

6 Then God said, "Let there be an expanse in the midst of the waters, and let it separate the waters from the waters."

7 God made the expanse, and separated the waters which were below the expanse from the waters which were above the expanse; and it was so.

8 God called the expanse heaven. And there was evening and there was morning, a second day.

9 Then God said, "Let the waters below the heavens be gathered into one place, and let the dry land appear"; and it was so.

10 God called the dry land earth, and the gathering of the waters He called seas; and God saw that it was good.

11 Then God said, "Let the earth sprout vegetation, plants yielding seed, and fruit trees on the earth bearing fruit after their kind with seed in them"; and it was so.

12 The earth brought forth vegetation, plants yielding seed after their kind, and trees bearing fruit with seed in them, after their kind; and God saw that it was good.

13 There was evening and there was morning, a third day.

14 Then God said, "Let there be lights in the expanse of the heavens to separate the day from the night, and let them be for signs and for seasons and for days and years;

15 and let them be for lights in the expanse of the heavens to give light on the earth"; and it was so.

16 God made the two great lights, the greater light to govern the day, and the lesser light to govern the night; He made the stars also.

17 God placed them in the expanse of the heavens to give light on the earth,

18 and to govern the day and the night, and to separate the light from the darkness; and God saw that it was good.

19 There was evening and there was morning, a fourth day.

20 Then God said, "Let the waters teem with swarms of living creatures, and let birds fly above the earth in the open expanse of the heavens."

VOICES
Hearing God
in a World of
Impostors

Old Testament

FYI:

The Trinity in Genesis

While some scholars believe the plural pronouns in Genesis ("us" in 1:26 and 3:22 and "our" in 1:26) refer either to God's majesty (as ancient kings often addressed themselves) or to angels (1 Kings 22:19-23), most conservative scholars believe this is an early reference to the Trinity.

---

21 God created the great sea monsters and every living creature that moves, with which the waters swarmed after their kind, and every winged bird after its kind; and God saw that it was good.

22 God blessed them, saying, "Be fruitful and multiply, and fill the waters in the seas, and let birds multiply on the earth."

23 There was evening and there was morning, a fifth day.

24 Then God said, "Let the earth bring forth living creatures after their kind: cattle and creeping things and beasts of the earth after their kind"; and it was so.

25 God made the beasts of the earth after their kind, and the cattle after their kind, and everything that creeps on the ground after its kind; and God saw that it was good.

26 Then God said, "Let Us make man in Our image, according to Our likeness; and let them rule over the fish of the sea and over the birds of the sky and over the cattle and over all the earth, and over every creeping thing that creeps on the earth."

27 God created man in His own image, in the image of God He created him; male and female He created them.

28 God blessed them; and God said to them, "Be fruitful and multiply, and fill the earth, and subdue it; and rule over the fish of the sea and over the birds of the sky and over every living thing that moves on the earth."

29 Then God said, "Behold, I have given you every plant yielding seed that is on the surface of all the earth, and every tree which has fruit yielding seed; it shall be food for you;

30 and to every beast of the earth and to every bird of the sky and to every thing that moves on the earth which has life, I have given every green plant for food"; and it was so.

31 God saw all that He had made, and behold, it was very good. And there was evening and there was morning, the sixth day.

DISCUSS with your GROUP or PONDER on your own . . .

Fill in this simple chart to record what God said, what happened, and how the results are described:

Verse	What God Said	What Happened	How it is Described

In summary, what happens when God speaks?

What and who does God bless?

What does God command? How do His commands tie in with the blessings?

What do we learn about God Himself from verse 26?

GOD CREATES, COMPLETES, AND RESTS

From your reading you'll recall that in Genesis 2:1-14, God completes His work, places man in Eden, and blesses the seventh day and rests on it.

OBSERVE the TEXT of SCRIPTURE

READ Genesis 2:15-18. **MARK** every reference to God speaking or commanding. **UNDERLINE** every instruction or command He gives.

Genesis 2:15-18

15 *Then the LORD God took the man and put him into the garden of Eden to cultivate it and keep it.*

16 *The LORD God commanded the man, saying, "From any tree of the garden you may eat freely;*

VOICES
HEARING GOD
IN A WORLD OF
IMPOSTORS

Old Testament

17 *but from the tree of the knowledge of good and evil you shall not eat, for in the day that you eat from it you will surely die."*

18 *Then the LORD God said, "It is not good for the man to be alone; I will make him a helper suitable for him."*

DISCUSS with your GROUP or PONDER on your own . . .

What does God command the man? Is He clear? What consequences does He lay out?

How restrictive is the command? Explain.

Is anything about God's voice unclear or ambiguous? Explain your answer.

IN THE GARDEN

At the end of Genesis 2, God creates the woman and brings her to the man.

OBSERVE the TEXT of SCRIPTURE

READ Genesis 3:1-5 and **MARK** every reference to the *serpent* including pronouns. **UNDERLINE** everything the serpent says.

Genesis 3:1-5

1 *Now the serpent was more crafty than any beast of the field which the LORD God had made. And he said to the woman, "Indeed, has God said, 'You shall not eat from any tree of the garden'?"*

2 *The woman said to the serpent, "From the fruit of the trees of the garden we may eat;*

3 but from the fruit of the tree which is in the middle of the garden, God has said, 'You shall not eat from it or touch it, or you will die.' "

4 The serpent said to the woman, "You surely will not die!

5 "For God knows that in the day you eat from it your eyes will be opened, and you will be like God, knowing good and evil."

DISCUSS with your GROUP or PONDER on your own . . .

Describe the serpent. How does the serpent engage the woman in conversation?

What is his point of attack? What does he call into question?

What lie does he tell the woman? Does he tell her any truth? If so, what?

Does anything the serpent says make God's words less clear? Explain.

Have you seen Satan mix truth and lies in our days? If so, how? How can you stand in the face of this kind of enemy?

FYI:

The Deceiver of the World
And the great dragon was thrown down, the serpent of old who is called the devil and Satan, who deceives the whole world; he was thrown down to the earth, and his angels were thrown down with him.

—Revelation 12:9

VOICES
HEARING GOD
IN A WORLD OF
IMPOSTORS

Old Testament

SIN ENTERS THE WORLD

The woman sees the fruit, desires it, takes it, eats it, and gives some to her husband. Their eyes are opened, they sew fig leaves together to cover themselves, and they hide when they hear God approaching.

ONE STEP FURTHER:

Word Study: Crafty

If you have time this week, find the Hebrew word that translates "crafty." Where else does it appear in the Old Testament and how is it typically used? For bonus points, see if you can find what root word it's associated with that appears elsewhere in the account of the fall. Record your findings below.

OBSERVE the TEXT of SCRIPTURE

READ Genesis 3:9-13. **MARK** every reference to *God* including pronouns.

Genesis 3:9-13

9 Then the LORD God called to the man, and said to him, "Where are you?"

10 He said, "I heard the sound of You in the garden, and I was afraid because I was naked; so I hid myself."

11 And He said, "Who told you that you were naked? Have you eaten from the tree of which I commanded you not to eat?"

12 The man said, "The woman whom You gave to be *with me,* she gave me from the tree, and I ate."

13 Then the LORD God said to the woman, "What is this you have done?" And the woman said, "The serpent deceived me, and I ate."

DISCUSS with your GROUP or PONDER on your own . . .

What questions does God ask the man?

What are the possible simple answers to "Have you eaten from the tree of which I commanded you not to eat?" What did the man include in his response and why do you think he did this?

Do you ever respond in a similar way? Explain.

What does God ask the woman? How does she respond?

Does the serpent still deceive today? How can we recognize his deception before it is too late? In order to help answer this, compare the voice of God and the voice of the serpent in Genesis 1–3.

What God Says	What the Serpent Says

FYI:

Clear or Crafty?
From the earliest chapters of the Bible, God speaks clear truth while Satan, who John calls "the serpent of old" (Revelation 12:9), craftily twists words. In his Gospel John also refers to Satan as the father of lies: "He was a murderer from the beginning, and does not stand in the truth because there is no truth in him. Whenever he speaks a lie, he speaks from his own *nature*, for he is a liar and the father of lies" (John 8:44b).

ONE STEP FURTHER:

Judging the Serpent
If you have some extra time this week, read Genesis 3:14-15 to see what God says to the serpent and how He judges him. Record your findings below.

Finally, looking back over all of Genesis 1–3 record all the texts that testify to God's goodness and care for His creation. When Eve went looking for something more, was it because God had not provided adequately? Explain your answer.

VOICES
HEARING GOD
IN A WORLD OF
IMPOSTORS

Old Testament

Digging Deeper

God's Judgment on Adam and Eve

God's judgment doesn't stop with the serpent. He follows through with Adam and Eve and their descendents (you and me) as well. If you have time this week look at God's words to Eve, to Adam, and at His summary of the state of affairs in Genesis 3:16-24.

Eve (Genesis 3:16)

How does God punish Eve?

Adam (Genesis 3:17-19)

What voice had Adam listened to instead of God's?

What judgment does he reap?

What other consequence comes because of Adam's sin?

The state of mankind (Genesis 3:21-24)

Was kicking them out of the garden a punishment or act of mercy? Explain.

How would you characterize Adam and Eve's various interactions with God? How did they change from the first time God spoke to Adam?

@THE END OF THE DAY . . .

Yes, we've only made it through Genesis 3! The first chapters of Genesis are critical in helping us understand not only how God speaks, but also how the adversary perverts and challenges truth. We'll pick up speed soon enough! For now, jot down the different contexts in which God spoke in the first three chapters of Genesis paying attention to what was positive and what was hard. Then, write down your biggest takeaway from this week of study.

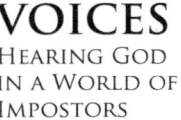

VOICES
HEARING GOD
IN A WORLD OF
IMPOSTORS

Week One: **What Voices are Calling?**

WEEK TWO

A God Who Calls Clearly

The unfolding of Your words gives light;
It gives understanding to the simple.
—Psalm 119:130

God spoke clearly to Adam. After placing the man in a garden paradise and providing for him bountifully, God gave one prohibition and clearly laid out the corresponding judgment. Still, the serpent called God's words and character into question and twisted the simple truth into a deadly lie. This week we'll continue to see God speaking to people in Genesis—men and women, rulers and slaves, from unrighteous Cain to Abraham who was called God's friend—in many portions and in many ways.

As you read, remember that the first five books of the Bible include two histories: when people did not have scriptures at all and when scriptures were first being recorded. Deuteronomy 31:24-26 tells us that Moses wrote the Torah—Genesis, Exodus, Leviticus, Numbers, and Deuteronomy—and Jesus affirms this in the New Testament.

Therefore, prior to Moses men and women had no written revelation to consult. This week we'll continue to look at other ways God spoke to people prior to revealing Himself through His written Word.

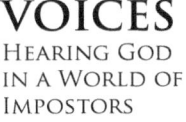

VOICES
HEARING GOD
IN A WORLD OF
IMPOSTORS

Old Testament

EXPELLED

God sends Adam and Eve out of the Garden and blocks the entrance with cherubim and a flaming sword.

OBSERVE the TEXT of SCRIPTURE

READ Genesis 4:1-16. **MARK** in distinct ways references to *Cain, Abel,* and *the LORD*.

Genesis 4:1-16

1 *Now the man had relations with his wife Eve, and she conceived and gave birth to Cain, and she said, "I have gotten a manchild with* the help of *the LORD."*

2 *Again, she gave birth to his brother Abel. And Abel was a keeper of flocks, but Cain was a tiller of the ground.*

3 *So it came about in the course of time that Cain brought an offering to the LORD of the fruit of the ground.*

4 *Abel, on his part also brought of the firstlings of his flock and of their fat portions. And the LORD had regard for Abel and for his offering;*

5 *but for Cain and for his offering He had no regard. So Cain became very angry and his countenance fell.*

6 *Then the LORD said to Cain, "Why are you angry? And why has your countenance fallen?*

7 *"If you do well, will not your countenance be lifted up? And if you do not do well, sin is crouching at the door; and its desire is for you, but you must master it."*

8 *Cain told Abel his brother. And it came about when they were in the field, that Cain rose up against Abel his brother and killed him.*

9 *Then the LORD said to Cain, "Where is Abel your brother?" And he said, "I do not know. Am I my brother's keeper?"*

10 *He said, "What have you done? The voice of your brother's blood is crying to Me from the ground.*

11 *"Now you are cursed from the ground, which has opened its mouth to receive your brother's blood from your hand.*

12 *"When you cultivate the ground, it will no longer yield its strength to you; you will be a vagrant and a wanderer on the earth."*

13 *Cain said to the LORD, "My punishment is too great to bear!*

14 *"Behold, You have driven me this day from the face of the ground; and from Your face I will be hidden, and I will be a vagrant and a wanderer on the earth, and whoever finds me will kill me."*

15 *So the LORD said to him, "Therefore whoever kills Cain, vengeance will be taken on him sevenfold." And the LORD appointed a sign for Cain, so that no one finding me would slay him.*

16 *Then Cain went out from the presence of the LORD, and settled in the land of Nod, east of Eden.*

ONE STEP FURTHER:

Word Study: Master

God tells Cain in Genesis 4:7 that he must "master" sin. If you have extra time and energy this week, find the Hebrew word that translates "master" and see how else it is used in the Torah and the rest of the Old Testament. Record your findings below.

VOICES

HEARING GOD
IN A WORLD OF
IMPOSTORS

Old Testament

DISCUSS with your GROUP or PONDER on your own . . .

Describe Abel and his offering. Then describe Cain and his offering.

Which offering does God accept? Does the text tell us why?

Which brother does God speak to? What is his emotional condition?

What three questions does God ask in verses 6-7?

What does God warn Cain? What additional challenge is there to Cain's obedience according to verse 7?

What does God tell Cain to do? Is He clear?

INDUCTIVE FOCUS:

What is a Key Word?

A key word or phrase unlocks the meaning of a text. Key words are usually repeated and are critical to understanding texts.

If a text references people, start your key word marking with them. In Genesis 4:1-16, we marked everything the text teaches about *Cain, Abel,* and the *LORD.*

Identifying key words is a skill that develops over time, but you practice by observing carefully so keep your eyes opened. You will get it; just keep praying and keep looking . . . and get started by marking the people you see!

FYI:

Kind Words; Hard Words

As we make our way through the Word, pay attention to the variety of messages. Unlike some modern writers would like you to believe, God's Words to man are not all warm and fuzzy. God's voice does bring words of comfort and peace, but it also brings words of warning and judgment. Our loving God is also holy and just.

VOICES

HEARING GOD
IN A WORLD OF
IMPOSTORS

Old Testament

What does Cain do after God speaks to him the first time?

ONE STEP FURTHER:

For More on Abel
For more on Abel, check out Hebrews 11:4 and 12:24 and see what is said about his blood. Record your findings below.

Compare God's approach to Cain after his sin with His approach to Adam and Eve after theirs.

What does God ask Cain this time? What does He follow up with?

How does Cain's answer differ from His parents'?

What punishment does God proclaim against Cain? How does Cain respond? What consequences does he acknowledge? What does he fear?

What specific protection does God provide?

Summarize God's interactions with Cain. Was God clear? Did Cain know what was expected? Why was he punished? What God was going to do for him?

LIFE OUTSIDE OF THE GARDEN

Sin abounds between the time of Cain and Noah with Enoch as the lone sparkle on the biblical landscape. He "walked with God; and he was not, for God took him." During this time frame, the Bible says nothing about God speaking but plots the decline of the human race until the time of Noah. You'll want to read the entire account of Noah in Genesis 6–9. Then we'll look more closely at some sections of the text together.

OBSERVE the TEXT of SCRIPTURE

READ Genesis 6:13-22. **MARK** in a distinctive way every reference to *God* and *Noah* (include pronouns).

Genesis 6:13-22

13 *Then God said to Noah, "The end of all flesh has come before Me; for the earth is filled with violence because of them; and behold, I am about to destroy them with the earth.*

14 *"Make for yourself an ark of gopher wood; you shall make the ark with rooms, and shall cover it inside and out with pitch.*

15 *"This is how you shall make it: the length of the ark three hundred cubits, its breadth fifty cubits, and its height thirty cubits.*

16 *"You shall make a window for the ark, and finish it to a cubit from the top; and set the door of the ark in the side of it; you shall make it with lower, second, and third decks.*

17 *"Behold, I, even I am bringing the flood of water upon the earth, to destroy all flesh in which is the breath of life, from under heaven; everything that is on the earth shall perish.*

18 *"But I will establish My covenant with you; and you shall enter the ark—you and your sons and your wife, and your sons' wives with you.*

19 *"And of every living thing of all flesh, you shall bring two of every kind into the ark, to keep them alive with you; they shall be male and female.*

20 *"Of the birds after their kind, and of the animals after their kind, of every creeping thing of the ground after its kind, two of every kind will come to you to keep them alive.*

21 *"As for you, take for yourself some of all food which is edible, and gather it to yourself; and it shall be for food for you and for them."*

22 *Thus Noah did; according to all that God had commanded him, so he did.*

INDUCTIVE FOCUS:

Using Cross-References
Although Enoch is barely a blip on the Genesis radar, we can discover a little more about him elsewhere in Scripture by searching on his name in an online concordance such as www.blueletterbible.org.

If you have some extra time this week, see where Enoch appears in Scripture and what the Word says about him. Record your findings below.

INDUCTIVE FOCUS:

Marking the Text
Marking the text helps us see what is important. By marking God and Noah in Genesis 6, we'll identify everything in the text that both God and Noah say and do. Do you need to mark the text to identify this information? Of course not, but marking slows us down and gives us visual clues so we don't overlook things.

VOICES
HEARING GOD
IN A WORLD OF
IMPOSTORS

Old Testament

DISCUSS with your GROUP or PONDER on your own . . .

What does God say and do?

Why does God say He will flood the earth? How clear is He?

What does God instruct Noah to do? What does He specifically command?

Describe Noah's response.

How are you at obeying the clear and revealed Word of God? Have you done *"according to all that God commanded"*? Explain.

What would you have to do to be more like Noah in this regard?

INDUCTIVE FOCUS:

Questioning the Text

The key to exegesis (the fancy word for drawing meaning out of Scripture) is questioning the text. The basic investigative questions *Who? What? When? Where? Why?* and *How?* are your framework. Not every question is answered by every verse, and many verses will take several questions formed from who, what, when, where, why or how to obtain comprehensive meaning. As we study God's Word together, realize that we will not ask every question that can be asked, but don't let that stop you from asking other questions and exploring further on your own. We will never run out of questions to ask and answers to glean from God's Word!

If you're at a loss for what questions to ask, pay attention to the key words that you've marked—including people, places, and timing—and start there with your questions! *Who is speaking or acting? Where are they? Why did this happen? etc.* Marking helps you see the main idea and ask questions.

COMING DESTRUCTION

Noah spent around 100 years constructing this ark. Even with an extended life span of several hundred years (which was common in those days), 100 years is a long obedience to a difficult task in a hostile environment.

OBSERVE the TEXT of SCRIPTURE

READ Genesis 7:1-5. **MARK** every number reference. Also keep your eyes opened for specific time phrases.

Genesis 7:1-5

1   Then the LORD said to Noah, "Enter the ark, you and all your household, for you alone I have seen to be righteous before Me in this time.

2   "You shall take with you of every clean animal by sevens, a male and his female; and of the animals that are not clean two, a male and his female;

3   also of the birds of the sky, by sevens, male and female, to keep offspring alive on the face of all the earth.

4   "For after seven more days, I will send rain on the earth forty days and forty nights; and I will blot out from the face of the land every living thing that I have made."

5   Noah did according to all that the LORD had commanded him.

DISCUSS with your GROUP or PONDER on your own . . .

Is God specific about the animals Noah is to bring? How many? What kinds?

What information does God give Noah about the duration and effect of the rain? Was this critical for Noah to know? Explain.

ONE STEP FURTHER:

Walked with God

What other biblical characters "walked with God"? What do we know about each of them? What does the phrase mean? How do those who walked with God contrast with their contemporaries? What does "walk with God" mean? Record your observations and conclusions below.

VOICES
HEARING GOD
IN A WORLD OF
IMPOSTORS

Old Testament

From other biblical accounts, does God always give timing information? Can you think of biblical examples of those who obeyed without answers to "How long?" and others, like Noah, who were given specific information? If so, write them down.

Are you ever slow to obey because you don't have the answer to "How long?" If so, why and in what type situations? Is "How long?" an answer that we typically need in order to obey? Support your answer from Scripture.

OBSERVE the TEXT of SCRIPTURE

READ Genesis 8:15–9:17. **MARK** every reference to *covenant.*

Genesis 8:15–9:17

15 *Then God spoke to Noah, saying,*

16 *"Go out of the ark, you and your wife and your sons and your sons' wives with you.*

17 *"Bring out with you every living thing of all flesh that is with you, birds and animals and every creeping thing that creeps on the earth, that they may breed abundantly on the earth, and be fruitful and multiply on the earth."*

18 *So Noah went out, and his sons and his wife and his sons' wives with him.*

19 *Every beast, every creeping thing, and every bird, everything that moves on the earth, went out by their families from the ark.*

20 *Then Noah built an altar to the LORD, and took of every clean animal and of every clean bird and offered burnt offerings on the altar.*

21 *The LORD smelled the soothing aroma; and the LORD said to Himself, "I will never again curse the ground on account of man, for the intent of man's heart is evil from his youth; and I will never again destroy every living thing, as I have done.*

22 *"While the earth remains,*

    Seedtime and harvest,

    And cold and heat,

    And summer and winter,

    And day and night

    Shall not cease."

9:1 *And God blessed Noah and his sons and said to them, "Be fruitful and multiply, and fill the earth.*

2 *"The fear of you and the terror of you will be on every beast of the earth and on every bird of the sky; with everything that creeps on the ground, and all the fish of the sea, into your hand they are given.*

3 *"Every moving thing that is alive shall be food for you; I give all to you, as I gave the green plant.*

4 *"Only you shall not eat flesh with its life, that is, its blood.*

5 *"Surely I will require your lifeblood; from every beast I will require it. And from every man, from every man's brother I will require the life of man.*

6 *"Whoever sheds man's blood,*

By man his blood shall be shed,

For in the image of God

He made man.

7 *"As for you, be fruitful and multiply;*

Populate the earth abundantly and multiply in it."

8 *Then God spoke to Noah and to his sons with him, saying,*

9 *"Now behold, I Myself do establish My covenant with you, and with your descendants after you;*

10 *and with every living creature that is with you, the birds, the cattle, and every beast of the earth with you; of all that comes out of the ark, even every beast of the earth.*

11 *"I establish My covenant with you; and all flesh shall never again be cut off by the water of the flood, neither shall there again be a flood to destroy the earth."*

12 *God said, "This is the sign of the covenant which I am making between Me and you and every living creature that is with you, for all successive generations;*

13 *I set My bow in the cloud, and it shall be for a sign of a covenant between Me and the earth.*

14 *"It shall come about, when I bring a cloud over the earth, that the bow will be seen in the cloud,*

15 *and I will remember My covenant, which is between Me and you and every living creature of all flesh; and never again shall the water become a flood to destroy all flesh.*

16 *"When the bow is in the cloud, then I will look upon it, to remember the everlasting covenant between God and every living creature of all flesh that is on the earth."*

17 *And God said to Noah, "This is the sign of the covenant which I have established between Me and all flesh that is on the earth."*

VOICES
HEARING GOD
IN A WORLD OF
IMPOSTORS

Old Testament

Week Two: **A God Who Calls Clearly**

DISCUSS with your GROUP or PONDER on your own . . .

After the flood, what does God tell Noah to do? Did He repeat any commands? If so, which one(s)?

FYI:

Another Word on Noah
By faith Noah, being warned by God about things not yet seen, in reverence prepared an ark for the salvation of his household, by which he condemned the world, and became an heir of the righteousness which is according to faith.

—Hebrews 11:7

What does God tell Noah about man's condition?

What can we learn from this? How can knowing this truth affect how we live?

What will stay the same? How does God confirm this? What will change?

Is He specific and clear? Explain.

Did you notice anything in this section that can apply to modern issues of morality? If so, explain.

A NEW BEGINNING

God spoke clearly and twice repeated to Noah the command He had spoken to Adam and Eve—be fruitful and multiply, and fill the earth. But did they?

OBSERVE the TEXT of SCRIPTURE

READ Genesis 11:1-9 and **MARK** every reference to the people of the earth. In this text, you'll be marking mostly pronouns—*they, us,* etc.

Genesis 11:1-9

1 *Now the whole earth used the same language and the same words.*

2 *It came about as they journeyed east, that they found a plain in the land of Shinar and settled there.*

3 *They said to one another, "Come, let us make bricks and burn them thoroughly." And they used brick for stone, and they used tar for mortar.*

4 *They said, "Come, let us build for ourselves a city, and a tower whose top will reach into heaven, and let us make for ourselves a name, otherwise we will be scattered abroad over the face of the whole earth."*

5 *The LORD came down to see the city and the tower which the sons of men had built.*

6 *The LORD said, "Behold, they are one people, and they all have the same language. And this is what they began to do, and now nothing which they purpose to do will be impossible for them.*

7 *"Come, let Us go down and there confuse their language, so that they will not understand one another's speech."*

8 *So the LORD scattered them abroad from there over the face of the whole earth; and they stopped building the city.*

9 *Therefore its name was called Babel, because there the LORD confused the language of the whole earth; and from there the LORD scattered them abroad over the face of the whole earth.*

DISCUSS with your GROUP or PONDER on your own . . .

Look back at what you've marked and describe the people.

What specific command do the people rebel against? How does God respond?

Was man able to thwart God's plan then? What about now?

FYI:

We Don't Need to Know Everything

When you want answers that aren't clearly given, remember Deuteronomy 29:29: "The secret things belong to God . . . ."

God has given us "everything that pertains to life and godliness" according to 2 Peter 1:3 and that is enough. Not everything needs to be revealed or explained.

Do you know God's revealed Word in the Bible well enough to know if you are obeying Him? Are there any specific commands that you know you are rebelling against? What changes could bring you more into alignment with God's revealed Word?

GOD SPEAKS TO ABRAM

The biblical text doesn't record instances of God speaking to people after the time of Noah until Abram appears on the scene. According to Genesis 11, Abram and his family were from Ur of the Chaldeans.

OBSERVE the TEXT of SCRIPTURE

READ Genesis 12:1-7. **UNDERLINE** God's command to Abram. **CIRCLE** every occurrence of *I will.*

Genesis 12:1-7

1 *Now the LORD said to Abram,*

   "Go forth from your country,

   And from your relatives

   And from your father's house,

   To the land which I will show you;

2 *And I will make you a great nation,*

   And I will bless you,

   And make your name great;

   And so you shall be a blessing;

3 *And I will bless those who bless you,*

   And the one who curses you I will curse.

   And in you all the families of the earth will be blessed."

4 *So Abram went forth as the LORD had spoken to him; and Lot went with him. Now Abram was seventy-five years old when he departed from Haran.*

5 *Abram took Sarai his wife and Lot his nephew, and all their possessions which they had accumulated, and the persons which they had acquired in Haran, and they set out for the land of Canaan; thus they came to the land of Canaan.*

6 *Abram passed through the land as far as the site of Shechem, to the oak of Moreh. Now the Canaanite was then in the land.*

7 *The LORD appeared to Abram and said, "To your descendants I will give this land." So he built an altar there to the LORD who had appeared to him.*

DISCUSS with your GROUP or PONDER on your own . . .

What does God specifically call Abram to do?

Does anything lack clarity? If so, what? Explain.

What does God promise to do for Abram?

How are you at obeying when you have only part of the information (or limited or incomplete information)? What can you learn from Abram's obedience?

INDUCTIVE FOCUS:

Marking Time Phrases

Abram's life gives a good example of how helpful it can be to mark time phrases. Genesis 12:4 tells us that Abram left Haran when he was 75 years old. Subsequent passages tell us what happens to him at other specific times in his life as well as what happens to his descendants for 400 years. Marking these references and other time phrases such as *before, after, then, when,* etc. can help you follow the timing of events.

FYI:

Abram's Roots in Ur

Abram traveled hundreds of miles in response to God's call first going to Haran and then to the Promised Land. While we know the land as Israel it was called Canaan during Abram's time.

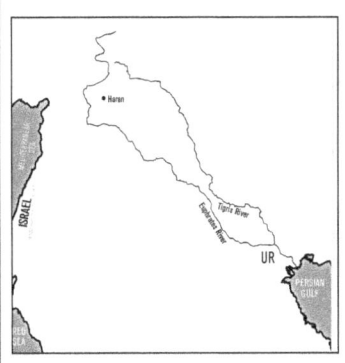

VOICES

HEARING GOD
IN A WORLD OF
IMPOSTORS

Old Testament

33

Digging Deeper

The Rest of the Story of Abraham

God spoke to Abraham at different points over the course of his life. We looked at the first time together and we'll look at another shortly. If you have time this week, check out other times God spoke to Abraham noting the increasing specificity of the promise in each encounter.

Genesis 13:14-17

Genesis 15

Genesis 16:16–18:33 (The LORD speaks to Sarah here, too!)

Genesis 21:12-13

ONE STEP FURTHER:

Joshua 24

This week get some more background information on Abraham and his family from the book of Joshua. See what you can find out about where he was from, what his religion was like, and anything else of relevance. Record your findings below.

A LONG HISTORY

By the time this next event takes place, God and Abraham have a long history together and God has dramatically clarified His promise. The verses in the **Digging Deeper** section will give you more information. (If you haven't tried a **Digging Deeper** section yet, this is a great place to start!)

OBSERVE the TEXT of SCRIPTURE

READ Genesis 22:1-18. **MARK** every reference to *Isaac*, including pronouns.

Genesis 22:1-18

1 Now it came about after these things, that God tested Abraham, and said to him, "Abraham!" And he said, "Here I am."

2 He said, "Take now your son, your only son, whom you love, Isaac, and go to the land of Moriah, and offer him there as a burnt offering on one of the mountains of which I will tell you."

3 So Abraham rose early in the morning and saddled his donkey, and took two of his young men with him and Isaac his son; and he split wood for the burnt offering, and arose and went to the place of which God had told him.

4 On the third day Abraham raised his eyes and saw the place from a distance.

5 Abraham said to his young men, "Stay here with the donkey, and I and the lad will go over there; and we will worship and return to you."

6 Abraham took the wood of the burnt offering and laid it on Isaac his son, and he took in his hand the fire and the knife. So the two of them walked on together.

7 Isaac spoke to Abraham his father and said, "My father!" And he said, "Here I am, my son." And he said, "Behold, the fire and the wood, but where is the lamb for the burnt offering?"

8 Abraham said, "God will provide for Himself the lamb for the burnt offering, my son." So the two of them walked on together.

9 Then they came to the place of which God had told him; and Abraham built the altar there and arranged the wood, and bound his son Isaac and laid him on the altar, on top of the wood.

10 Abraham stretched out his hand and took the knife to slay his son.

11 But the angel of the LORD called to him from heaven and said, "Abraham, Abraham!" And he said, "Here I am."

12 He said, "Do not stretch out your hand against the lad, and do nothing to him; for now I know that you fear God, since you have not withheld your son, your only son, from Me."

13 Then Abraham raised his eyes and looked, and behold, behind him a ram caught in the thicket by his horns; and Abraham went and took the ram and offered him up for a burnt offering in the place of his son.

14 Abraham called the name of that place The LORD Will Provide, as it is said to this day, "In the mount of the LORD it will be provided."

15 Then the angel of the LORD called to Abraham a second time from heaven,

16 and said, "By Myself I have sworn, declares the LORD, because you have done this thing and have not withheld your son, your only son,

17 indeed I will greatly bless you, and I will greatly multiply your seed as the stars of the heavens and as the sand which is on the seashore; and your seed shall possess the gate of their enemies.

18 "In your seed all the nations of the earth shall be blessed, because you have obeyed My voice."

ONE STEP FURTHER:

Credited as Righteousness

While God commends Abraham's obedience in Genesis 22:18, we see in Genesis 15 that God credited righteousness to Abraham on the basis of his belief. Take some time this week to examine both Genesis 15:6 and Paul's quotation of it in Romans 4. Consider how faith and action relate in these verses (and elsewhere in Scripture if you choose) and record your observations below.

VOICES
HEARING GOD
IN A WORLD OF
IMPOSTORS

Old Testament

DISCUSS with your GROUP or PONDER on your own . . .

Describe Isaac from the text.

INDUCTIVE FOCUS:

Scripture Interprets Scripture

The commentary of Hebrews 11:17-19 on the sacrifice of Isaac provides one of the best illustrations of Scripture interpreting Scripture:

By faith Abraham, when he was tested, offered up Isaac, and he who had received the promises was offering up his only begotten son; it was he to whom it was said, "IN ISAAC YOUR DESCENDANTS SHALL BE CALLED." He considered that God is able to raise people even from the dead, from which he also received him back as a type.

What does God tell Abraham to do? What is not revealed but will be? Does it sound like a previous command? If so, which one?

What two-fold promise has God already made to Abraham?

If you didn't do the **Digging Deeper** section, be sure to check out Genesis 15:6 to see what the text says about Abraham's belief in what God promised and record your findings.

How specific has the promise become according to Genesis 21:12-13? What did God add to His original promise in Genesis 12:1-3?

What does Abraham's obedience show us about his view of God's character? What does He expect God to do based on His promise? Does He expect Him to default?

When you are in situations that call for difficult obedience, how can knowing God's voice through His Word help you to stand?

Digging Deeper

Hagar and Abimelech

God did not limit His communication to patriarchs and other Old Testament big-wigs. If you have extra time this week, look at how He communicates twice with an Egyptian woman named Hagar and then a Philistine king named Abimelech. As you look at each encounter ask the 5 W and H questions and note the response of the person involved and the clarity of God's Word to each one. Record your observations and comparisons.

God speaks to Hagar . . .
Genesis 16:7-13

Genesis 21:1-21

God speaks to Abimelech . . .
Genesis 20:3-7

How do these accounts compare with one another? How do they compare with other instances of God speaking to people throughout Genesis?

ONE STEP FURTHER:

God Leads Abraham's Servant
If you have some extra time this week, read the Genesis 24 account of Abraham's servant's search for a wife for Isaac. Note how God leads this praying man even without speaking audibly to Him. Record your findings below.

ISAAC GROWS UP

In Genesis 22 God asked Abraham to sacrifice his only son, Isaac, on Mount Moriah. Abraham obeyed fully, but God sent an angel to stop him from harming the young man. In Genesis 24 Abraham sends his trusted servant back to the land of his relatives to find a wife for Isaac. The promise to Abraham will continue to Isaac and Jacob.

Unlike his father and mother, Isaac turned to God on behalf of his barren wife Rebekah. God answered him and blessed them with twin sons. The first record of God speaking to Isaac, however, comes in Genesis 26.

OBSERVE the TEXT of SCRIPTURE

READ Genesis 26:1-6. **MARK** every reference to the *LORD*, including pronouns, and **UNDERLINE** everything He says to Isaac.

Genesis 26:1-6

1 *Now there was a famine in the land, besides the previous famine that had occurred in the days of Abraham. So Isaac went to Gerar, to Abimelech king of the Philistines.*

2 *The LORD appeared to him and said, "Do not go down to Egypt; stay in the land of which I shall tell you.*

3 *"Sojourn in this land and I will be with you and bless you, for to you and to your descendants I will give all these lands, and I will establish the oath which I swore to your father Abraham.*

4 *"I will multiply your descendants as the stars of heaven, and will give your descendants all these lands; and by your descendants all the nations of the earth shall be blessed;*

5 *because Abraham obeyed Me and kept My charge, My commandments, My statutes and My laws."*

6 *So Isaac lived in Gerar.*

DISCUSS with your GROUP or PONDER on your own . . .

Where has Isaac gone and why according to verse 1?

When God appears to him, what does He tell him not to do? Why? What's implied, given the current events?

What does God tell him to do instead? Where specifically does He tell Isaac to be? Is this clear?

ONE STEP FURTHER:

More Words to Isaac

During his time among the Philistines, Isaac repeats his father's "this-is-my-sister" deception and then has a conflict with the locals over some wells that he had dug. God appears to him again at Beersheba in Genesis 26:19-25.

If you have time this week, check out this encounter. Record below what God said to Isaac. Was He clear? How does this compare with what He had told his father Abraham?

What else does He tell Isaac? How does this compare with His words to Abraham?

How does Isaac respond?

Have you ever found yourself waiting out a "famine"? How did you do? What truths sustain you during trying times?

JACOB FLEES AND GOD SPEAKS

The Bible tells us far more about Abraham and Jacob than Isaac. As far as we know from the text, God first speaks to Jacob when he is an adult traveling from the land of Canaan toward his relatives in Aram. He is both fleeing from his enraged brother and going to the house of his relatives to find a suitable wife.

OBSERVE the TEXT of SCRIPTURE

READ Genesis 28:10-17. **MARK** every reference to *God* and **UNDERLINE** everything He says to Jacob.

Genesis 28:10-17

10 Then Jacob departed from Beersheba and went toward Haran.

11 He came to a certain place and spent the night there, because the sun had set; and he took one of the stones of the place and put it under his head, and lay down in that place.

12 He had a dream, and behold, a ladder was set on the earth with its top reaching to heaven; and behold, the angels of God were ascending and descending on it.

13 And behold, the LORD stood above it and said, "I am the LORD, the God of your father Abraham and the God of Isaac; the land on which you lie, I will give it to you and to your descendants.

ONE STEP FURTHER:

God Answers Rebekah

God spoke to both Abraham and Sarah in Genesis 18 when He appeared by the oaks of Mamre. In Genesis 25:23 He speaks to their daughter-in-law, Rebekah, If you have time this week, read Genesis 25:19-34 for yourself and ask the 5 Ws and H.

Here are a few questions to get you started:

• *What answer to prayer had God already given Isaac?*

• *What did Rebekah inquire of God?*

• *What does it mean to "inquire" (Hebrew: daras) of God?*

• *What answer did God give her?*

• *How was it confirmed?*

Record your answers and observations below.

VOICES

HEARING GOD
IN A WORLD OF
IMPOSTORS

FYI:

Dream

While God brought a deep sleep *(tardemah)* on Abram (Genesis 15:12), Jacob's dream in Genesis 28:12 is the first of 29 Old Testament occurrences of the Hebrew word *chalam*, here translated "dream."

FYI:

Aram and Canaan

Jacob headed northeast out of the land of Canaan when he left Beersheba going toward Haran and finally settled in Paddan-aram with his uncle Laban.

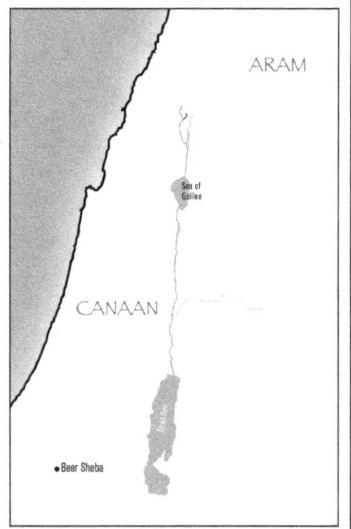

FYI:

Playing for Keeps

Now to Him who is able to keep you from stumbling, and to make you stand in the presence of His glory blameless with great joy, to the only God our Savior, through Jesus Christ our Lord, be glory, majesty, dominion and authority, before all time and now and forever. Amen.

—Jude 24-25

14 *"Your descendants will also be like the dust of the earth, and you will spread out to the west and to the east and to the north and to the south; and in you and in your descendants shall all the families of the earth be blessed.*

15 *"Behold, I am with you and will keep you wherever you go, and will bring you back to this land; for I will not leave you until I have done what I have promised you."*

16 *Then Jacob awoke from his sleep and said, "Surely the LORD is in this place, and I did not know it."*

17 *He was afraid and said, "How awesome is this place! This is none other than the house of God, and this is the gate of heaven."*

DISCUSS with your GROUP or PONDER on your own . . .

Where does this event take place? What other geographic markers does the text give?

How does God speak to Jacob? Compare this with accounts we've seen so far.

What does God tell Jacob? List the specifics.

How does this compare with what He has said to Abraham and Isaac? What do each of these encounters have to do with God's plan of salvation? Cite your references.

What new word does He give Jacob? (Watch how this truth sustains Jacob when he faces challenging times.)

How does this promise compare with what believers have today?

What security does His keeping power give? How can you apply this truth in your life?

"GO HOME"

After Jacob spends 20+ years with Laban, marrying two of his daughters and working for him, the LORD tells him to go back home.

OBSERVE the TEXT of SCRIPTURE

READ Genesis 31:1-3 and **MARK** every reference to *Jacob.*

Genesis 31:1-3

1 *Now Jacob heard the words of Laban's sons, saying, "Jacob has taken away all that was our father's, and from what belonged to our father he has made all this wealth."*

2 *Jacob saw the attitude of Laban, and behold, it was not friendly toward him as formerly.*

3 *Then the LORD said to Jacob, "Return to the land of your fathers and to your relatives, and I will be with you."*

FYI:

Jacob Informs His Wives

While Genesis 31:3 says that the LORD told Jacob to return to the land of his fathers, Genesis 31:11-13, gives more details. As Jacob tells his wives Rachel and Leah his plans for them all to leave, he explains that God spoke to him in a dream: "Then the angel of God said to me in the dream, 'Jacob,' and I said, 'Here I am.' He said, 'Lift up now your eyes and see that all the male goats which are mating are striped, speckled, and mottled; for I have seen all that Laban has been doing to you. 'I am the God of Bethel, where you anointed a pillar, where you made a vow to Me; now arise, leave this land, and return to the land of your birth.'"

ONE STEP FURTHER:

Laban's Dream

How does Laban's dream coincide with what God was doing with Jacob? Read the account in Genesis 31:24 and record your findings below.

VOICES
HEARING GOD
IN A WORLD OF
IMPOSTORS

Old Testament

DISCUSS with your GROUP or PONDER on your own . . .

How has Jacob's situation changed over the years?

ONE STEP FURTHER:

His Eyes are on You, Too

God tells Jacob *I have seen all that Laban has been doing to you* (Genesis 31:12). He gives Jacob new information about Himself that is not recorded until Moses writes it down. Today we know that God not only watched Jacob and Laban but that He also sees all things. If you have some time this week, search the Bible for this truth of God's omniscience. Jacob needed a dream to get this information from God, but God has had it written down for us!

What difference can the truth of His omniscience make in your life this week?

When does God speak to him? What does He say? How specific is He?

How does Jacob's moving back to Canaan relate to God's promise?

Take a moment to assess the consistency of God's message to Abraham, Isaac and Jacob. How does this consistency encourage you?

RETURNING AS A HOUSEHOLD

Jacob had left his homeland alone, on the run from his offended brother and searching for a proper wife. He returns with two wives and two concubines in tow along with an entire household as he approaches the territory of the brother who wanted him dead.

VOICES
HEARING GOD
IN A WORLD OF
IMPOSTORS

Old Testament

OBSERVE the TEXT of SCRIPTURE

READ all of Genesis 32 in your Bible. Then **READ** Genesis 32:24-32 and **UNDERLINE** everything Jacob says. **BOX** everything his wrestling opponent says.

Genesis 32:24-32

24 Then Jacob was left alone, and a man wrestled with him until daybreak.

25 When he saw that he had not prevailed against him, he touched the socket of his thigh; so the socket of Jacob's thigh was dislocated while he wrestled with him.

26 Then he said, "Let me go, for the dawn is breaking." But he said, "I will not let you go unless you bless me."

27 So he said to him, "What is your name?" And he said, "Jacob."

28 He said, "Your name shall no longer be Jacob, but Israel; for you have striven with God and with men and have prevailed."

29 Then Jacob asked him and said, "Please tell me your name." But he said, "Why is it that you ask my name?" And he blessed him there.

30 So Jacob named the place Peniel, for he said, "I have seen God face to face, yet my life has been preserved."

31 Now the sun rose upon him just as he crossed over Penuel, and he was limping on his thigh.

32 Therefore, to this day the sons of Israel do not eat the sinew of the hip which is on the socket of the thigh, because he touched the socket of Jacob's thigh in the sinew of the hip.

DISCUSS with your GROUP or PONDER on your own . . .

How does Jacob address God in verse 9? How does he address God—whose God is He? What promise does Jacob remind God of in verse 12?

What happens to Jacob the night before he encounters Esau? Where is he? Who is he with? What does he do?

ONE STEP FURTHER:

God's Camp

Now as Jacob went on his way, the angels of God met him. Jacob said when he saw them, 'This is God's camp.' So he named that place Mahanaim.

—Genesis 32:1-2

If you have time this week, take notes as you read Genesis 32 to set the context for Jacob's wrestling match in verses 24-32. It is a difficult passage for sure, and with difficult passages the more context the better!

Remember to ask the 5Ws and H and then record your observations below.

FYI:

Wrestling at the Jabbok

As Jacob approached Esau's land (Edom), his wrestling match took place by the Jabbok River.

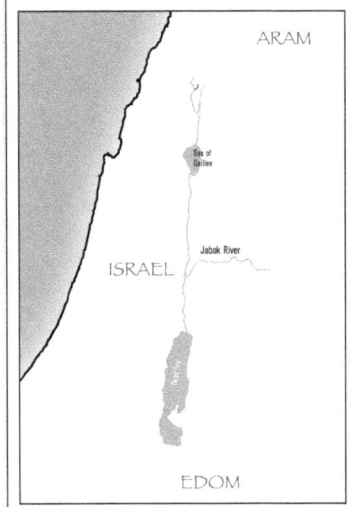

VOICES

HEARING GOD IN A WORLD OF IMPOSTORS

Old Testament

43

Week Two: **A God Who Calls Clearly**

Describe the conversation at daybreak recorded in Genesis 32:24-32. What two-fold request does Jacob make? What does he get?

Does he get the information he asks for? What does he receive? Explain.

How does Jacob interpret this encounter? Explain.

How had God spoken with Jacob in the past?

What tangible evidence shows that this was more than a dream? In what way does Jacob come out of this encounter weakened? Conversely, how does he emerge strengthened?

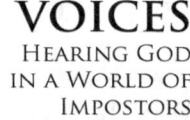

Digging Deeper

The Rest of the Story of Jacob

Want more of Jacob's story? Here are other accounts where God spoke to him. As you read, remember to ask: What does God say? How specific is He? Is He clear? Is He consistent? Does Jacob clearly know what is required? Record your findings below.

Genesis 35.1-3

Genesis 35:9-15

Genesis 46:1-5

Summary of general observations:

Descriptive or Prescriptive

As we read Old Testament accounts of God speaking to individuals, we need to remember that Hebrews tells us that God spoke long ago "in many portions and in many ways" and that "in these last days He has spoken in His Son."

Descriptions are not prescriptions. For example, God established the priesthood, but He ordained only Aaron's line to serve as priests. When Korah and his ilk tried to assert themselves as priests, God judged them (Numbers 16). The priesthood was described and established as good, but it was not prescribed for those not descended from Aaron.

Similarly here, a description of God speaking through dreams to Jacob and Joseph is not a prescription for believers today who have the indwelling Holy Spirit to seek similar experiences.

JOSEPH'S DREAMS

Abraham was asleep on one occasion when God spoke to him (Genesis 15:12ff), but the LORD also showed up at his doorstep. The Hebrew term for "dream" (*chalam*) is used for the first time with reference to Jacob (Genesis 28:12) but appears throughout the account of Joseph. Joseph was the eleventh of Jacob's twelve sons and the first-born son of his favored wife, Rachel.

VOICES
HEARING GOD
IN A WORLD OF
IMPOSTORS

OBSERVE the TEXT of SCRIPTURE

READ Genesis 37:3-11. **MARK** every occurrence of *dream*, including pronouns.

Genesis 37:3-11

3 Now Israel loved Joseph more than all his sons, because he was the son of his old age; and he made him a varicolored tunic.

4 His brothers saw that their father loved him more than all his brothers; and so they hated him and could not speak to him on friendly terms.

5 Then Joseph had a dream, and when he told it to his brothers, they hated him even more.

6 He said to them, "Please listen to this dream which I have had;

7 for behold, we were binding sheaves in the field, and lo, my sheaf rose up and also stood erect; and behold, your sheaves gathered around and bowed down to my sheaf."

8 Then his brothers said to him, "Are you actually going to reign over us? Or are you really going to rule over us?" So they hated him even more for his dreams and for his words.

9 Now he had still another dream, and related it to his brothers, and said, "Lo, I have had still another dream; and behold, the sun and the moon and eleven stars were bowing down to me."

10 He related it to his father and to his brothers; and his father rebuked him and said to him, "What is this dream that you have had? Shall I and your mother and your brothers actually come to bow ourselves down before you to the ground?"

11 His brothers were jealous of him, but his father kept the saying in mind.

DISCUSS with your GROUP or PONDER on your own . . .

Describe Joseph's relationships with his father and brothers.

Thinking back to Jacob's life, what was a key component in Jacob's hearing from God?

What does Joseph dream about according to Genesis 37? How do his dreams differ from his father's?

How do his brothers react to the dreams? How does his father respond?

THE LORD WAS WITH HIM

Genesis 39 tells us that God was with Joseph and that others saw that the LORD was with him and caused what he did to prosper. The favored son of Jacob, Joseph was held in such disdain by his brothers that they sold him into Egyptian slavery. After running the household of a prominent Egyptian, Joseph lands in prison after being falsely accused of attempted rape.

OBSERVE the TEXT of SCRIPTURE

READ Genesis 40:1-13, 16-22. **UNDERLINE** every occurrence of *dream*. **CIRCLE** every occurrence of *interpret/interpretation(s)*.

Genesis 40:1-13

1 *Then it came about after these things, the cupbearer and the baker for the king of Egypt offended their lord, the king of Egypt.*

2 *Pharaoh was furious with his two officials, the chief cupbearer and the chief baker.*

3 *So he put them in confinement in the house of the captain of the bodyguard, in the jail, the same place where Joseph was imprisoned.*

4 *The captain of the bodyguard put Joseph in charge of them, and he took care of them; and they were in confinement for some time.*

5 *Then the cupbearer and the baker for the king of Egypt, who were confined in jail, both had a dream the same night, each man with his own dream and each dream with its own interpretation.*

6 *When Joseph came to them in the morning and observed them, behold, they were dejected.*

7 *He asked Pharaoh's officials who were with him in confinement in his master's house, "Why are your faces so sad today?"*

8 *Then they said to him, "We have had a dream and there is no one to interpret it." Then Joseph said to them, "Do not interpretations belong to God? Tell it to me, please."*

9 *So the chief cupbearer told his dream to Joseph, and said to him, "In my dream, behold, there was a vine in front of me;*

10 *and on the vine were three branches. And as it was budding, its blossoms came out, and its clusters produced ripe grapes.*

11 *"Now Pharaoh's cup was in my hand; so I took the grapes and squeezed them into Pharaoh's cup, and I put the cup into Pharaoh's hand."*

12 *Then Joseph said to him, "This is the interpretation of it: the three branches are three days;*

13 *within three more days Pharaoh will lift up your head and restore you to your office; and you will put Pharaoh's cup into his hand according to your former custom when you were his cupbearer.*

Genesis 40:16-22

16 *When the chief baker saw that he had interpreted favorably, he said to Joseph, "I also saw in my dream, and behold, there were three baskets of white bread on my head;*

17 *and in the top basket there were some of all sorts of baked food for Pharaoh, and the birds were eating them out of the basket on my head."*

18 *Then Joseph answered and said, "This is its interpretation: the three baskets are three days;*

19 *within three more days Pharaoh will lift up your head from you and will hang you on a tree, and the birds will eat your flesh off you."*

20 *Thus it came about on the third day, which was Pharaoh's birthday, that he made a feast for all his servants; and he lifted up the head of the chief cupbearer and the head of the chief baker among his servants.*

21 *He restored the chief cupbearer to his office, and he put the cup into Pharaoh's hand;*

22 *but he hanged the chief baker, just as Joseph had interpreted to them.*

DISCUSS with your GROUP or PONDER on your own . . .

Where does Joseph meet the King's cupbearer and baker? How long had they been there prior to having their dreams?

What was significant about the timing of the two dreams? What effect do the dreams have on the men?

Why? How does Joseph get involved? According to Joseph, why is he able to interpret the dreams?

How is Joseph's interpretive gift proved true? How do subsequent facts authenticate his interpretations?

PHARAOH HAS A DREAM

In accordance with the dream, the cupbearer is released from prison but he forgets Joseph until two years later when Pharaoh has a dream . . .

OBSERVE the TEXT of SCRIPTURE

READ all of Genesis 41. Then, **MARK** every reference to *God* in Genesis 41:25-32.

Genesis 41:25-32

25 Now Joseph said to Pharaoh, "Pharaoh's dreams are one and the same; *God has told to Pharaoh what He is about to do.*

26 "The seven good cows are seven years; and the seven good ears are seven years; the dreams are one and the same.

27 "The seven lean and ugly cows that came up after them are seven years, and the seven thin ears scorched by the east wind will be seven years of famine.

28 "It is as I have spoken to Pharaoh: *God has shown to Pharaoh what He is about to do.*

29 "Behold, seven years of great abundance are coming in all the land of Egypt;

30 and after them seven years of famine will come, and all the abundance will be forgotten in the land of Egypt, and the famine will ravage the land.

31 "So the abundance will be unknown in the land because of that subsequent famine; for it will be very severe.

32 "Now as for the repeating of the dream to Pharaoh twice, it means *that the matter is determined by God, and God will quickly bring it about.*

DISCUSS with your GROUP or PONDER on your own . . .

When is Pharaoh's dream relative to the cupbearer's and baker's? How many times does he dream? Describe each dream.

How does his post-dream condition compare with that of the cupbearer and baker?

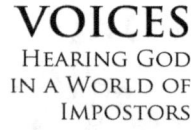

VOICES
HEARING GOD
IN A WORLD OF
IMPOSTORS

Old Testament

Why does Pharaoh call for Joseph? How has God orchestrated the series of events?

How does Joseph explain his ability to explain Pharaoh's dream?

What is Joseph's interpretation? How does Pharaoh respond?

How does Pharaoh's dream fit in with the larger biblical narrative? How do the events it predicts fit in with what will happen to Joseph's family in the coming years?

Week Two: **A God Who Calls Clearly**

@THE END OF THE DAY . . .

As we close out our week of study, take some time to synthesize and summarize what you've learned so far about God's sovereignty over revelation. When did God speak? Under what kinds of circumstances? Did He bring good news, bad news, or a mix? Were His words hard or easy? Clear or cryptic? At whose initiative did He speak and for what purpose? Once you've thought these things through and jotted down your responses, be sure to record your biggest takeaway from this week of study. What have you learned that will change the way you think and act?

WEEK THREE
Write this in a Book

When He had finished speaking with him upon Mount Sinai,
He gave Moses the two tablets of the testimony,
tablets of stone, written by the finger of God.

—Exodus 31:18

The pages of Genesis record God's active involvement in His creation. As the letter to the Hebrews reminds us "He spoke in many portions and in many ways" and while the Bible doesn't always tell us exactly *how* He spoke, it tells us *what* we need to know—God communicated clearly to people: sometimes they understood it; sometimes they chose not to. At times He spoke clearly in dreams while other dreamers needed a prophet like Joseph to put (God's) words to the "visions" they saw, but in all cases God's communication was clear. As we move into Exodus, God and His prophets begin to write. God Himself writes the ten commandments on tablets of stone (Exodus 31:18; 34:1). Later, His prophet Moses records the Law for Israel (Exodus 17:14; 34:27).

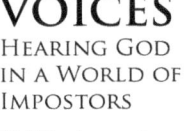

FROM JOSEPH TO MOSES

When Joseph interprets Pharaoh's God-sent dream warning about an impending famine, Pharaoh listens and takes action. He promotes Joseph to second in command over all of Egypt and tasks him with preparing the nation.

Joseph then administrates the food handling during both the seven years of abundance and the seven years of famine. During the famine, Joseph's family relocates to Egypt and lives well until Joseph dies and a new Pharaoh arises who doesn't "remember" him.

The opening verses of Exodus recount a startling turn of events by human standards but one which God had clearly foretold to Abraham. Fearing the ever-multiplying Hebrew population might side with an invader, the Egyptians enslave the Hebrews and eventually begin killing their male babies. Moses is born against this backdrop. Exodus 2 ends with the people crying out to God because of their bondage and the text says, "God saw the sons of Israel, and God took notice *of them.*" During this time of outcry to God, Moses has been in the land of Midian. We'll pick up his story in Exodus 3.

OBSERVE the TEXT of SCRIPTURE

READ Exodus 3–4 and answer the discussion questions below.

DISCUSS with your GROUP or PONDER on your own . . .

Exodus 3 Questions

What does Moses notice as he pastures Jethro's flock? How does he respond?

How does God call to Moses? What does He say? How does He identify Himself? What continuity is there with the Genesis narrative? Whose God is he?

What objections does Moses have? What does he ask God? How does God answer each of his questions?

ONE STEP FURTHER:

Super Clear

If you have some extra time this week, check out the clear words God gave Abraham in Genesis 15:13-16 regarding his descendants' future enslavement. Jot down the details below and note how the prophecy is fulfilled in the early chapters of Exodus.

INDUCTIVE FOCUS:

Marking the Text

Throughout the workbook you'll notice suggestions for ways to **mark** key words in the text. Remember, these are suggestions. **Marking** the text will help key words stand out and the method of **marking** you use (if you choose to **mark** at all) is entirely up to you. In this section of the text, you may find it helpful to highlight God's words to Moses in one color and Moses' objections in another. It will help you see the flow of the conversation.

Always remember that **marking** is a means to understanding the text, not an end in itself.

What does God tell Moses to do in verses 16-17? What does He tell Moses in advance about how the people and Pharaoh will respond and about how everything will turn out? Are His words confusing or clear?

Word Study: Appeared

If you have time this week, examine the word "appeared" with reference to God appearing to men. How is the word used of God? Of others? Record your findings below.

Exodus 4 Questions

What does Moses object to according to verse 1? Is the objection realistic given what God has already clearly told him? How does God respond?

The Moses Bio

Born into Egyptian slavery, Moses escaped death as an infant during a time when a fearful Pharaoh was having male Hebrew babies killed. His mother, obeying the letter of the law, cast him into the Nile River in a pitched-covered basket—literally translated an "ark." After being drawn from the water and given the name Moses (which means "drawn from the water"), Moses grew up in Pharaoh's household as the son of Pharaoh's daughter.

What are Moses' final objections and God's responses? What additional clear instructions does God give Moses in Exodus 4?

Scripture tells us in Acts 7 that "when he was approaching the age of 40" he went out to look on his Hebrew brothers and killed an Egyptian who was beating one of his kinsmen. He then fled to the land of Midian where he married the daughter of Jethro, priest of Midian, and shepherded his flock for the next 40 years.

Who else does God talk to in Exodus 4? What does He say?

Moses' life can be divided in three distinct 40-year sections: 40 years in Egypt; 40 years in Midian; and 40 years serving as God's deliverer for His people. The final 40-year segment kicks off in Exodus 3.

How does God authenticate His words at the end of Exodus 4?

Do you ever squirm away from the clear Word of God in the way Moses did? Explain. If you do squirm, what biblical correctives can you bring to this kind of behavior?

VOICES
HEARING GOD
IN A WORLD OF
IMPOSTORS

Digging Deeper

Read Exodus

If you're up for some extra work this week, read or listen to the entire book of Exodus noting God's specific words and the shift toward written communication.

In what different ways does God communicate with His people throughout the book of Exodus?

Where in Exodus does God give specific instructions? Record significant sections and the type of specific instructions He gives.

Compare the way God communicates in Genesis and Exodus. What similarities did you notice? What differences?

FYI:

A Tale of Two Pharaohs

God used a listening Pharaoh to bring his people to Egypt for safety during a time of famine. Later He delivered them from another Pharaoh—one who denied the One True God.

Joseph's Pharaoh . . .

So Pharaoh said to Joseph, "Since God has informed you of all this, there is no one so discerning and wise as you are. "You shall be over my house, and according to your command all my people shall do homage; only in the throne I will be greater than you." Pharaoh said to Joseph, "See, I have set you over all the land of Egypt."

—Genesis 41:39-41

Moses' Pharaoh . . .

And afterward Moses and Aaron came and said to Pharaoh, "Thus says the LORD, the God of Israel, 'Let My people go that they may celebrate a feast to Me in the wilderness.' " But Pharaoh said, "Who is the LORD that I should obey His voice to let Israel go? I do not know the LORD, and besides, I will not let Israel go."

—Exodus 5:1-2

TWO KINDS OF PHARAOHS

In Genesis, God communicated to a responsive Pharaoh in a dream. Exodus paints the picture of a Pharaoh with stopped-up ears. In both cases God communicated with men, but the responses of the men led to radically different results.

OBSERVE the TEXT of SCRIPTURE

READ Exodus 5:1-9 and **MARK** every reference to *Pharaoh* including pronouns.

Exodus 5:1-9

1 And afterward Moses and Aaron came and said to Pharaoh, "Thus says the LORD, the God of Israel, 'Let My people go that they may celebrate a feast to Me in the wilderness.' "

2 But Pharaoh said, "Who is the LORD that I should obey His voice to let Israel go? I do not know the LORD, and besides, I will not let Israel go."

3 Then they said, "The God of the Hebrews has met with us. Please, let us go a three days' journey into the wilderness that we may sacrifice to the LORD our God, otherwise He will fall upon us with pestilence or with the sword."

4 But the king of Egypt said to them, "Moses and Aaron, why do you draw the people away from their work? Get back to your labors!"

5 *Again Pharaoh said, "Look, the people of the land are now many, and you would have them cease from their labors!"*

6 *So the same day Pharaoh commanded the taskmasters over the people and their foremen, saying,*

7 *"You are no longer to give the people straw to make brick as previously; let them go and gather straw for themselves.*

8 *"But the quota of bricks which they were making previously, you shall impose on them; you are not to reduce any of it. Because they are lazy, therefore they cry out, 'Let us go and sacrifice to our God.'*

9 *"Let the labor be heavier on the men, and let them work at it so that they will pay no attention to false words."*

DISCUSS with your GROUP or PONDER on your own . . .

How does Pharaoh react to the message from God? What are his specific objections—what won't he do and why?

How does Pharaoh characterize God's voice? How does Pharaoh's view of God affect his actions?

What does Pharaoh accuse Moses and Aaron of doing? How does he specifically characterize their words in verse 9?

What difference did knowing or not knowing God's voice make for Moses and Pharaoh? What difference does it make today?

ONE STEP
FURTHER:

Earnest Heed to God's Voice
How often does Exodus refer to God's voice? Find the Hebrew word that translates "voice" and compare how it is used throughout the book. Record your findings below.

VOICES
HEARING GOD
IN A WORLD OF
IMPOSTORS

Old Testament

57

OPPRESSION AND HEARING IMPAIRMENT

When Pharaoh further oppresses the Hebrews, the people stop listening to Moses for a time.

FYI:

Under Compulsion

The Hebrew phrase *yad* (hand) *hazaq* (strength) appears twice in Exodus 6:1, translated as "under compulsion" in the NASB, but more literally in the ESV: "But the LORD said to Moses, 'Now you shall see what I will do to Pharaoh; for with a *strong hand* he will send them out, and with a *strong hand* he will drive them out of his land'."

ONE STEP FURTHER:

And They Will Know

If you have some extra time this week, trace the phrases "you will know that I am the LORD" and "they will know that I am the LORD" through Exodus. Who is God talking about? How will the people know? What will God do to communicate this truth? Record your findings below.

OBSERVE the TEXT of SCRIPTURE

READ Exodus 6:1-11. **MARK** every occurrence of *spoke*, *said*, or *say*.

Exodus 6:1-11

1   Then the LORD said to Moses, "Now you shall see what I will do to Pharaoh; for under compulsion he will let them go, and under compulsion he will drive them out of his land."

2   God spoke further to Moses and said to him, "I am the LORD;

3   and I appeared to Abraham, Isaac, and Jacob, as God Almighty, but by *My name, LORD, I did not make Myself known to them.*

4   "I also established My covenant with them, to give them the land of Canaan, the land in which they sojourned.

5   "Furthermore I have heard the groaning of the sons of Israel, because the Egyptians are holding them in bondage, and I have remembered My covenant.

6   "Say, therefore, to the sons of Israel, 'I am the LORD, and I will bring you out from under the burdens of the Egyptians, and I will deliver you from their bondage. I will also redeem you with an outstretched arm and with great judgments.

7   'Then I will take you for My people, and I will be your God; and you shall know that I am the LORD your God, who brought you out from under the burdens of the Egyptians.

8   'I will bring you to the land which I swore to give to Abraham, Isaac, and Jacob, and I will give it to you for a possession; I am the LORD.' "

9   So Moses spoke thus to the sons of Israel, but they did not listen to Moses on account of their *despondency and cruel bondage.*

10 Now the LORD spoke to Moses, saying,

11 "Go, tell Pharaoh king of Egypt to let the sons of Israel go out of his land."

DISCUSS with your GROUP or PONDER on your own . . .

According to the LORD, how will Pharaoh let the people go?

What does God say about Himself in this section? How does this tie in with what He says in Genesis?

What is unique about God's appearance to Moses? What has God "remembered" and why is it significant?

What does God tell Moses to tell the people about who He is and what He will do? What will the people know as a result?

Do the people listen? Why/why not? What are some reasons people are unable to listen to God today?

ONE STEP FURTHER:

Other Signs

Miraculous events alone don't verify a person or message as being from God. If you have some time this week, examine the signs and wonders that the Egyptian magicians produced. Here are a few questions to get you started: What signs were the magicians able to replicate? When did *they* realize God was involved? What can we learn from this to apply today? Record your findings below.

SPEAKING and LEADING

God continues to speak with Moses as the children of Israel escape Egypt and journey through the wilderness. He leads them by a pillar of cloud during the day and a pillar of fire at night. Throughout the book of Exodus God gives Moses specific commands he in turn gives to the people. In the next section of text we'll look at, the children of Israel encounter a bitter water situation which leads to instruction on listening to the voice of God.

VOICES

HEARING GOD
IN A WORLD OF
IMPOSTORS

Week Three: **Write this in a Book**

OBSERVE the TEXT of SCRIPTURE

READ Exodus 15:22-26. **MARK** every reference to the people and to the LORD. In both cases include pronouns.

Exodus 15:22-26

22 Then Moses led Israel from the Red Sea, and they went out into the wilderness of Shur; and they went three days in the wilderness and found no water.

23 When they came to Marah, they could not drink the waters of Marah, for they were bitter; therefore it was named Marah.

24 So the people grumbled at Moses, saying, "What shall we drink?"

25 Then he cried out to the LORD, and the LORD showed him a tree; and he threw it into the waters, and the waters became sweet. There He made for them a statute and regulation, and there He tested them.

26 And He said, "If you will give earnest heed to the voice of the LORD your God, and do what is right in His sight, and give ear to His commandments, and keep all His statutes, I will put none of the diseases on you which I have put on the Egyptians; for I, the LORD, am your healer."

ONE STEP FURTHER:

Clear Instructions on Food

If you have some extra time this week, read Exodus 16 to see God's clear instructions on food and what happened when the people did not obey. Record your observations below and consider what similarly clear instructions you botch from time to time.

DISCUSS with your GROUP or PONDER on your own . . .

What is Israel's need and how does God meet it? What does God say about listening to His voice? How does verse 26 help define God's voice?

In what ways do we forget or miss the voice of God when we grumble? Can you think of ways to correct this in your life this week?

WRITE IT DOWN

Trusting God for food and water proves to be an ongoing challenge to the Israelites even when God gives clear instructions and shows Himself faithful time and again. He continues to show His faithfulness during their first military battle which takes place when the Amalekites seek them out. After the battle against the Amalekites, we see the first instance of God instructing Moses to write something down.

OBSERVE the TEXT of SCRIPTURE

READ Exodus 17:8-14. **UNDERLINE** the two commandments God gives to Moses.

Exodus 17:8-14

8 *Then Amalek came and fought against Israel at Rephidim.*

9 *So Moses said to Joshua, "Choose men for us and go out, fight against Amalek. Tomorrow I will station myself on the top of the hill with the staff of God in my hand."*

10 *Joshua did as Moses told him, and fought against Amalek; and Moses, Aaron, and Hur went up to the top of the hill.*

11 *So it came about when Moses held his hand up, that Israel prevailed, and when he let his hand down, Amalek prevailed.*

12 *But Moses' hands were heavy. Then they took a stone and put it under him, and he sat on it; and Aaron and Hur supported his hands, one on one side and one on the other. Thus his hands were steady until the sun set.*

13 *So Joshua overwhelmed Amalek and his people with the edge of the sword.*

14 *Then the LORD said to Moses, "Write this in a book as a memorial and recite it to Joshua, that I will utterly blot out the memory of Amalek from under heaven."*

DISCUSS with your GROUP or PONDER on your own . . .

Describe the battle situation of Exodus 17 and Joshua's role in it.

What does God command Moses after the battle? Why? For who?

WRITE SOME MORE

While the words to Joshua are the first instance of God commanding Moses to write something down, Exodus records more instances of God either writing for Moses or Moses recording God's words for the people. Let's look at some of these together.

ONE STEP FURTHER:

Does God speak through normal people?

In Exodus 18, Moses' father-in-law Jethro instructs him how to better judge the people so that he and they won't wear themselves out. If you have extra time this week, read this account and record what Moses learns through this man.

It's not common for people today to say "God spoke to me through so and so." Let's think through this carefully: Does God use Jethro's "counsel" (18:19) to help Moses? Does this advice differ from God's direct communication to Moses? Is there a qualitative difference between this "counsel" and the content revealed to Moses? Explain your reasoning and think through any implications this might have on how you communicate in your everyday life. Record your observations and conclusions below.

VOICES
Hearing God
in a World of
Impostors

Old Testament

Week Three: **Write this in a Book**

OBSERVE the TEXT of SCRIPTURE

READ Exodus 19–20. Exodus 24:4 says that Moses recounted all of the words of the LORD to the people and wrote them down.

DISCUSS with your GROUP or PONDER on your own . . .

What is the setting of Exodus 19 and 20? What does God say to the people in this section? How do they respond?

What do we learn about God's holiness from this section of the text?

In what way does God set Moses apart from everyone else?

DRAWING NEAR

In Exodus 21–23 God speaks one long discourse to Moses to convey to His people. The words are clear and exceptionally specific. As Exodus 24 opens, the LORD calls Moses and the leaders to Him, but not everyone is allowed to come near. Let's look at the text together.

OBSERVE the TEXT of SCRIPTURE

READ Exodus 24:1-13. **UNDERLINE** every reference to the *words of the LORD* and anything God speaks. **CIRCLE** any references to the words being written down (*wrote, book,* etc.)

Exodus 24:1-13

1   *Then He said to Moses, "Come up to the LORD, you and Aaron, Nadab and Abihu and seventy of the elders of Israel, and you shall worship at a distance.*

2   *"Moses alone, however, shall come near to the LORD, but they shall not come near, nor shall the people come up with him."*

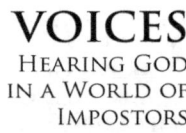

3   Then Moses came and recounted to the people all the words of the LORD and all the ordinances; and all the people answered with one voice and said, "All the words which the LORD has spoken we will do!"

4   Moses wrote down all the words of the LORD. Then he arose early in the morning, and built an altar at the foot of the mountain with twelve pillars for the twelve tribes of Israel.

5   He sent young men of the sons of Israel, and they offered burnt offerings and sacrificed young bulls as peace offerings to the LORD.

6   Moses took half of the blood and put it in basins, and the other half of the blood he sprinkled on the altar.

7   Then he took the book of the covenant and read it in the hearing of the people; and they said, "All that the LORD has spoken we will do, and we will be obedient!"

8   So Moses took the blood and sprinkled it on the people, and said, "Behold the blood of the covenant, which the LORD has made with you in accordance with all these words."

9   Then Moses went up with Aaron, Nadab and Abihu, and seventy of the elders of Israel,

10 and they saw the God of Israel; and under His feet there appeared to be a pavement of sapphire, as clear as the sky itself.

11 Yet He did not stretch out His hand against the nobles of the sons of Israel; and they saw God, and they ate and drank.

12 Now the LORD said to Moses, "Come up to Me on the mountain and remain there, and I will give you the stone tablets with the law and the commandment which I have written for their instruction."

13 So Moses arose with Joshua his servant, and Moses went up to the mountain of God.

DISCUSS with your GROUP or PONDER on your own . . .

Who are allowed to draw closer to God than the people at large? How is Moses distinguished from this group?

When God speaks to Moses, what does Moses do? How do the people respond? What do they commit to do?

ONE STEP FURTHER:

More Specifics
If you have time this week, read God's crystal clear directives in Exodus 25–29. Jot your findings below.

Week Three: **Write this in a Book**

What does the LORD give Moses on the mountain? What value is put on the written Word in this text? Explain.

Does writing clarify content and reduce transmission error? If so, how?

What value do you place on the written Word of God? How does your life show it?

SPECIFIC INSTRUCTIONS ON MEETING AND WORSHIP

In Exodus through Joshua, God communicated primarily with Moses and Joshua. Many of those interactions took place at the tent of meeting.

In Exodus 25–29 God gives specific instructions for constructing the tabernacle and carrying out appropriate worship. In Exodus 29:42-46 He explains the sacrifices that must be offered so that the people can meet with Him at the tent.

OBSERVE the TEXT of SCRIPTURE

READ Exodus 29:42-46 and **CIRCLE** every occurrence of the phrase *I will*. **UNDERLINE** *tent of meeting*.

Exodus 29:42-46

42 *"It shall be a continual burnt offering throughout your generations at the doorway of the tent of meeting before the LORD, where I will meet with you, to speak to you there.*

43 *"I will meet there with the sons of Israel, and it shall be consecrated by My glory.*

44 *"I will consecrate the tent of meeting and the altar; I will also consecrate Aaron and his sons to minister as priests to Me.*

45 *"I will dwell among the sons of Israel and will be their God.*

46 *"They shall know that I am the LORD their God who brought them out of the land of Egypt, that I might dwell among them; I am the LORD their God.*

DISCUSS with your GROUP or PONDER on your own . . .

What was the tent of meeting's purpose? Who specifically will the LORD meet with? Where will He dwell?

What will the people know? How will they know it?

How is God's relationship with the people changing? When was the last time in Scripture we saw people dwelling in His presence? Explain.

ONE STEP FURTHER:

Write
If you have time this week, search for the Hebrew words that are translated write/written. Where is the first time they are used? In what contexts do they occur? Record your findings below.

WRITTEN BY THE FINGER OF GOD

God continues to give Moses specifics about tabernacle worship and living in the presence of His holiness. This extended section of text where God speaks concludes at Exodus 31:18.

OBSERVE the TEXT of SCRIPTURE

READ Exodus 31:18 and **MARK** the two forms of communication mentioned.

Exodus 31:18

18 *When He had finished speaking with him upon Mount Sinai, He gave Moses the two tablets of the testimony, tablets of stone, written by the finger of God.*

Week Three: **Write this in a Book**

DISCUSS with your GROUP or PONDER on your own . . .

What two forms of communication does God use on the mountain with Moses?

Who wrote on the tablets? Why is this significant?

What benefits does written communication have over spoken words for future generations?

LISTENING TO THEMSELVES

While Moses is on the mountain receiving the spoken and written Words of God, the people start listening to their own voices.

OBSERVE the TEXT of SCRIPTURE

READ Exodus 32 identifying other voices that contradict God.

DISCUSS with your GROUP or PONDER on your own . . .

What do the people say to Aaron in Exodus 32:1? What does Aaron do and say in response?

How does their behavior deviate from the clear word of God? Does your behavior ever deviate from the clear Word of God? How? How can you correct this?

FORGIVENESS AND THE PRIESTHOOD

Although Aaron listens to the people's voices and consequently rebels, God mercifully forgives him and makes him the high priest of His people. Still, it is Moses, not Aaron, who God speaks to directly.

OBSERVE the TEXT of SCRIPTURE

READ Exodus 33:7-11. **MARK** every reference the *tent of meeting*.

Exodus 33:7-11

7 *Now Moses used to take the tent and pitch it outside the camp, a good distance from the camp, and he called it the tent of meeting. And everyone who sought the LORD would go out to the tent of meeting which was outside the camp.*

8 *And it came about, whenever Moses went out to the tent, that all the people would arise and stand, each at the entrance of his tent, and gaze after Moses until he entered the tent.*

9 *Whenever Moses entered the tent, the pillar of cloud would descend and stand at the entrance of the tent; and the LORD would speak with Moses.*

10 *When all the people saw the pillar of cloud standing at the entrance of the tent, all the people would arise and worship, each at the entrance of his tent.*

11 *Thus the LORD used to speak to Moses face to face, just as a man speaks to his friend. When Moses returned to the camp, his servant Joshua, the son of Nun, a young man, would not depart from the tent.*

DISCUSS with your GROUP or PONDER on your own . . .

Where was the tent of meeting located? Why would someone go to the tent?

How did God speak to Moses? According to Numbers 12:6-8 and Deuteronomy 34:10 how did this differ from other prophets "since"?

ONE STEP FURTHER:

Resisting the Clear Word

If you have some extra time this week, think through other biblical characters who resisted the clear word of God and record their names and stories below. We'll make our way to many of them as we study, but it's always good to think and reason through the Scriptures for yourself.

VOICES
HEARING GOD
IN A WORLD OF
IMPOSTORS

NOTES

GOD PASSES BY MOSES

While still in the wilderness, Moses tells God that he does not want to go further if His presence will not go with them. He then asks God to show him His glory. As the following text shows, even though Moses had a unique, face-to-face relationship with God, God's glory is unapproachable (1 Tim. 6:16). By this time, Moses had destroyed the original tablets in anger over Aaron and the people's sin.

OBSERVE the TEXT of SCRIPTURE

READ Exodus 33:17–34:8 and **MARK** every reference to *the LORD* including pronouns.

Exodus 33:17-23

17 The LORD said to Moses, *"I will also do this thing of which you have spoken; for you have found favor in My sight and I have known you by name."*

18 Then Moses said, *"I pray You, show me Your glory!"*

19 And He said, *"I Myself will make all My goodness pass before you, and will proclaim the name of the LORD before you; and I will be gracious to whom I will be gracious, and will show compassion on whom I will show compassion."*

20 But He said, *"You cannot see My face, for no man can see Me and live!"*

21 Then the LORD said, *"Behold, there is a place by Me, and you shall stand there on the rock;*

22 *and it will come about, while My glory is passing by, that I will put you in the cleft of the rock and cover you with My hand until I have passed by.*

23 *"Then I will take My hand away and you shall see My back, but My face shall not be seen."*

Exodus 34:1-8

1 Now the LORD said to Moses, *"Cut out for yourself two stone tablets like the former ones, and I will write on the tablets the words that were on the former tablets which you shattered.*

2 *"So be ready by morning, and come up in the morning to Mount Sinai, and present yourself there to Me on the top of the mountain.*

3 *"No man is to come up with you, nor let any man be seen anywhere on the mountain; even the flocks and the herds may not graze in front of that mountain."*

4 *So he cut out two stone tablets like the former ones, and Moses rose up early in the morning and went up to Mount Sinai, as the LORD had commanded him, and he took two stone tablets in his hand.*

5 *The LORD descended in the cloud and stood there with him as he called upon the name of the LORD.*

ONE STEP FURTHER:

Word Study: Glory

If you have some time this week, examine both the Old and New Testament words for glory—*kavod* (Hebrew) and *doxa* (Greek). Record your findings below.

ONE STEP FURTHER:

Covenant and Continuity

If you have some extra time this week, find the Hebrew word that translates "covenant" in the Old Testament and the Greek word that translates it in the New Testament. Then use your concordance to see how these words are used across the pages of Scripture paying attention to the continuity over time. Record your findings below.

6 *Then the LORD passed by in front of him and proclaimed, "The LORD, the LORD God, compassionate and gracious, slow to anger, and abounding in lovingkindness and truth;*

7 *who keeps lovingkindness for thousands, who forgives iniquity, transgression and sin; yet He will by no means leave the guilty unpunished, visiting the iniquity of fathers on the children and on the grandchildren to the third and fourth generations."*

8 *Moses made haste to bow low toward the earth and worship.*

DISCUSS with your GROUP or PONDER on your own . . .

What does Moses ask for in verse 18? Thinking back, what had he already seen of God by this point?

How does God respond? What will He reveal of Himself to Moses? When God passes in front of Moses, what does He declare about Himself? How does Moses respond?

How does God's self-description help you? What false thinking, if any, can it help to correct in your mind?

WRITE SOME MORE

After God passes before Moses and declares His name to him, Moses bows in worship and asks God to go with them in their midst, to pardon them and to take them as His own possession. God responds beginning in Exodus 34:10.

ONE STEP FURTHER:

Leading in the Wilderness
If you have some extra time this week, read Exodus 40:33-38 and describe how God led the people in the wilderness.

VOICES
HEARING GOD
IN A WORLD OF
IMPOSTORS

Old Testament

OBSERVE the TEXT of SCRIPTURE

READ Exodus 34:10-27, then in the verse 27 below, **MARK** every reference to *write* and *words*.

Exodus 34:27

27   Then the LORD said to Moses, *"Write down these words, for in accordance with these words I have made a covenant with you and with Israel."*

DISCUSS with your GROUP or PONDER on your own . . .

What does God say He is going to make with the people of Israel? What is He going to do before them and why? What does He warn against and why?

What does He tell Moses to do in Exodus 34:27? What is the covenant made in accordance with?

Was it important for the people to obey God's Words then? What did it involve then? What does it involve now? Explain.

QUOTING THE VERY WORDS OF GOD

Of the books of Moses, indeed of all the biblical books, none has a higher percentage of direct quotations from the mouth of God than Leviticus. None. Not even close! While God commanded many sacrificial rituals that have been fulfilled in the person and work of Jesus Christ, we're going to look at specific teaching regarding the tent of meeting and the holiness of God, listening to God's clear voice and rejecting the voices of impostors.

OBSERVE the TEXT of SCRIPTURE

READ Leviticus 9:23–10:3, 8-11. **MARK** every reference to *tent of meeting* and every reference to *the LORD*.

Leviticus 9:23–24 10:3, 8-11

23 *Moses and Aaron went into the tent of meeting. When they came out and blessed the people, the glory of the LORD appeared to all the people.*

24 *Then fire came out from before the LORD and consumed the burnt offering and the portions of fat on the altar; and when all the people saw it, they shouted and fell on their faces.*

Leviticus 10:1-3

1 *Now Nadab and Abihu, the sons of Aaron, took their respective firepans, and after putting fire in them, placed incense on it and offered strange fire before the LORD, which He had not commanded them.*

2 *And fire came out from the presence of the LORD and consumed them, and they died before the LORD.*

3 *Then Moses said to Aaron, "It is what the LORD spoke, saying, 'By those who come near Me I will be treated as holy, and before all the people I will be honored.' " So Aaron, therefore, kept silent.*

8 *The LORD then spoke to Aaron, saying,*

9 *"Do not drink wine or strong drink, neither you nor your sons with you, when you come into the tent of meeting, so that you will not die—it is a perpetual statute throughout your generations—*

10 *and so as to make a distinction between the holy and the profane, and between the unclean and the clean,*

11 *and so as to teach the sons of Israel all the statutes which the LORD has spoken to them through Moses."*

DISCUSS with your GROUP or PONDER on your own . . .

At the end of Leviticus 9, who is in the tent of meeting and what happens? How do the people react? Is there any doubt about the Lord's presence in this place?

What happens to Aaron's sons according to Leviticus 10:1? In offering "strange fire," how were they treating God?

Week Three: **Write this in a Book**

Remembering what you've read so far in Exodus and Leviticus, has God been clear regarding how the people are to worship? Explain.

ONE STEP FURTHER:

Word Studies: Mediums and Spiritists

If you have some extra time this week, see what Hebrew words translate "mediums" and "spiritists." Then, using your concordance see what else the Scriptures have to say about them. Record your findings below.

Who does God speak to after these two sons of Aaron die? What does He tell him? Would you consider it a reprimand or a warning? Explain.

What can we learn about God from this text? What applications can we make with regard to ways to approach and worship God today? Does anything go? Why/why not?

MEDIUMS AND SPIRITISTS

God clearly instructs His people and warns them not to seek words from others who defile and deceive. Not all who offer knowledge are of God. Remember the serpent . . .

OBSERVE the TEXT of SCRIPTURE

READ Leviticus 19:31, 20:6-7, 27 and **MARK** the words *mediums* and *spiritists*.

Leviticus 19:31

31 *'Do not turn to mediums or spiritists; do not seek them out to be defiled by them. I am the LORD your God.*

Leviticus 20:6-7, 27

 6 *'As for the person who turns to mediums and to spiritists, to play the harlot after them, I will also set My face against that person and will cut him off from among his people.*

 7 *'You shall consecrate yourselves therefore and be holy, for I am the LORD your God.*

27 *'Now a man or a woman who is a medium or a spiritist shall surely be put to death. They shall be stoned with stones, their bloodguiltiness is upon them.' "*

DISCUSS with your GROUP or PONDER on your own . . .

What voices does God specifically tell His people not to consult? What consequences will turning to these people bring? How will God judge their sin?

How are the people to punish this sin? How should they be behaving instead? Why?

In what ways do people today violate this command? What does violating this command say about a person's view of God and His voice? Explain.

A CONTINUING PATTERN OF COMMUNICATION

The early chapters of Numbers record God's command to number the people and recount His instructions regarding holy living. God gives very clear, very specific instructions regarding the priesthood and even how the camp of Israel should be organized. Throughout Numbers God establishes a specific manner of worship for His people. Let's look at a couple more instances of God speaking to Moses in the tent of meeting.

OBSERVE the TEXT of SCRIPTURE

READ the following passages and **MARK** every reference to the *tent of meeting* or the *tabernacle*.

Numbers 1:1-3

1 *Then the LORD spoke to Moses in the wilderness of Sinai, in the tent of meeting, on the first of the second month, in the second year after they had come out of the land of Egypt, saying,*

2 *"Take a census of all the congregation of the sons of Israel, by their families, by their fathers' households, according to the number of names, every male, head by head*

3 *from twenty years old and upward, whoever is able to go out to war in Israel, you and Aaron shall number them by their armies.*

VOICES
HEARING GOD
IN A WORLD OF
IMPOSTORS

Week Three: **Write this in a Book**

Numbers 7:89

89 *Now when Moses went into the tent of meeting to speak with Him, he heard the voice speaking to him from above the mercy seat that was on the ark of the testimony, from between the two cherubim, so He spoke to him.*

DISCUSS with your GROUP or PONDER on your own . . .

Where does God speak to Moses in these passages? What specifics does Numbers 7:89 give?

How does this compare with what we've seen so far? Explain.

ONE STEP FURTHER:

Caleb

While grumblers abound in the wilderness generation, Caleb believes God's promises and encourages others to stand on them too. If you have some extra time this week check out his story beginning in Numbers 13. Record your findings below.

Digging Deeper

Dissenting Voices

If you have some extra time this week, think through the first five books of the Bible, the Torah, and consider some of the human voices who, because of unbelief, opposed God's prophet Moses in the wilderness. Here are a few that you might want to consider.

Wilderness Grumblers

Numbers 12

Numbers 14

OBSERVE the TEXT of SCRIPTURE

READ Deuteronomy 13:1-5. **MARK** every reference to *dreams, dreamer,* and *prophet.*

Deuteronomy 13:1-5

1 *"If a prophet or a dreamer of dreams arises among you and gives you a sign or a wonder,*

2 *and the sign or the wonder comes true, concerning which he spoke to you, saying, 'Let us go after other gods (whom you have not known) and let us serve them,'*

3 *you shall not listen to the words of that prophet or that dreamer of dreams; for the LORD your God is testing you to find out if you love the LORD your God with all your heart and with all your soul.*

4 *"You shall follow the LORD your God and fear Him; and you shall keep His commandments, listen to His voice, serve Him, and cling to Him.*

5 *"But that prophet or that dreamer of dreams shall be put to death, because he has counseled rebellion against the LORD your God who brought you from the land of Egypt and redeemed you from the house of slavery, to seduce you from the way in which the LORD your God commanded you to walk. So you shall purge the evil from among you.*

DISCUSS with your GROUP or PONDER on your own . . .

Make a list of everything the text says about dreamers and prophets.

Does the ability to perform a "sign or wonder" confirm a prophet or dreamer as having a true message? Why/why not?

When confronted with "signs and wonders" and a message that contradicts God's Word, what are we to do?

VOICES
HEARING GOD
IN A WORLD OF
IMPOSTORS

Old Testament

75

Week Three: **Write this in a Book**

What does this presuppose? What do we need to know if we are going to distinguish truth from error? Where do we find it?

OBSERVE the TEXT of SCRIPTURE

READ Deuteronomy 18:9-22. **MARK** every reference to *listen* and *hear*.

Deuteronomy 18:9-22

9 *"When you enter the land which the LORD your God gives you, you shall not learn to imitate the detestable things of those nations.*

10 *"There shall not be found among you anyone who makes his son or his daughter pass through the fire, one who uses divination, one who practices witchcraft, or one who interprets omens, or a sorcerer,*

11 *or one who casts a spell, or a medium, or a spiritist, or one who calls up the dead.*

12 *"For whoever does these things is detestable to the LORD; and because of these detestable things the LORD your God will drive them out before you.*

13 *"You shall be blameless before the LORD your God.*

14 *"For those nations, which you shall dispossess, listen to those who practice witchcraft and to diviners, but as for you, the LORD your God has not allowed you to do so.*

15 *"The LORD your God will raise up for you a prophet like me from among you, from your countrymen, you shall listen to him.*

16 *"This is according to all that you asked of the LORD your God in Horeb on the day of the assembly, saying, 'Let me not hear again the voice of the LORD my God, let me not see this great fire anymore, or I will die.'*

17 *"The LORD said to me, 'They have spoken well.*

18 *'I will raise up a prophet from among their countrymen like you, and I will put My words in his mouth, and he shall speak to them all that I command him.*

19 *'It shall come about that whoever will not listen to My words which he shall speak in My name, I Myself will require it of him.*

20 *'But the prophet who speaks a word presumptuously in My name which I have not commanded him to speak, or which he speaks in the name of other gods, that prophet shall die.'*

21 *"You may say in your heart, 'How will we know the word which the LORD has not spoken?'*

22 *"When a prophet speaks in the name of the LORD, if the thing does not come about or come true, that is the thing which the LORD has not spoken. The prophet has spoken it presumptuously; you shall not be afraid of him.*

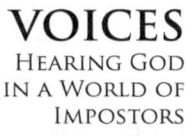

DISCUSS with your GROUP or PONDER on your own . . .

For what practices was God driving out the people of the land? What was Israel doing that it was forbidden to do? How are the practices described? What do these practices seek to find out?

Who do the nations listen to? Who are God's people to listen to?

What was to happen to prophets who attributed words to God that God did not command them to speak? How could the people determine if God had spoken?

How big of a deal was it to utter the words "Thus saith the Lord"?

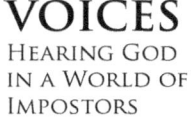

VOICES
Hearing God
in a World of
Impostors

Old Testament

Week Three: **Write this in a Book**

How much reverence do we exhibit when speaking "in God's name"? Do we put things in the mouth of God that have not been revealed in Scripture? Is this a proper practice? Why/why not?

OBSERVE the TEXT of SCRIPTURE

READ Deuteronomy 31:9-13. **MARK** references to *wrote* and *read*.

Deuteronomy 31:9-13

9 *So Moses wrote this law and gave it to the priests, the sons of Levi who carried the ark of the covenant of the LORD, and to all the elders of Israel.*

10 *Then Moses commanded them, saying, "At the end of every seven years, at the time of the year of remission of debts, at the Feast of Booths,*

11 *when all Israel comes to appear before the LORD your God at the place which He will choose, you shall read this law in front of all Israel in their hearing.*

12 *"Assemble the people, the men and the women and children and the alien who is in your town, so that they may hear and learn and fear the LORD your God, and be careful to observe all the words of this law.*

13 *"Their children, who have not known, will hear and learn to fear the LORD your God, as long as you live on the land which you are about to cross the Jordan to possess."*

DISCUSS with your GROUP or PONDER on your own . . .

After Moses wrote down the words of the law, who did he give it to and what did he command?

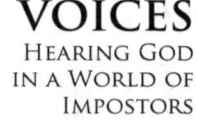

How often was the law to be read? Who was to hear it? What was the purpose of assembling the people to hear? How would this affect the children?

If you want to learn about and fear the LORD your God today, what can you do?

@THE END OF THE DAY . . .

Take a moment to think through everything you've learned thus far about how God spoke in the pages of the Torah. Summarize your thoughts below in a few short sentences. Then make a list of any questions you still have remaining, remembering that God has revealed much but not everything. Deuteronomy 29:29 tells us "The secret things belong to the LORD our God, but the things revealed belong to us and to our sons forever, that we may observe all the words of this law."

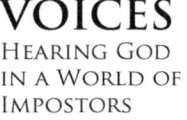

Week Three: **Write this in a Book**

WEEK FOUR

From Hearing to Deafness

Only be strong and very courageous;
be careful to do according to all the law which Moses
My servant commanded you; do not turn from it to the
right or to the left, so that you may have
success wherever you go.
—Joshua 1:7

With the death of Moses and the rise of Joshua as the flesh and blood leader of His people, God continues to anchor and authenticate His Word. Like Moses, Joshua continues to receive clear direct revelation from God and more and more we see this revelation being written down, eventually incorporated into manuscripts and books. Still, even in the face of specific, detailed, recorded information, the majority of God's people rebels against His call and purpose and becomes spiritually deaf.

REVIEW

Let's take a few minutes to review what we've learned about God speaking so far. Considering the Torah (Genesis through Deuteronomy) think through *who* God spoke to, *what* the circumstances were, *where* He spoke, *when* He spoke, *why* He spoke and *how* He spoke to people. Be brief, but use specific examples and cite your references.

In the beginning . . .

To the Patriarchs . . .

To Moses . . .

To Others . . .

The Major Shift in Exodus . . .

ACCORDING TO ALL THAT IS WRITTEN

Joshua is Israel's first leader to have a "Book." While God communicates information to him beyond Moses' writings, He stresses with both Joshua and the people the importance of the written commands. Let's take a look.

OBSERVE the TEXT of SCRIPTURE

READ Joshua 1:2-9. **MARK** every reference to *the law* and *the book of the law* including pronouns.

Joshua 1:2-9

2 *"Moses My servant is dead; now therefore arise, cross this Jordan, you and all this people, to the land which I am giving to them, to the sons of Israel.*

3 *"Every place on which the sole of your foot treads, I have given it to you, just as I spoke to Moses.*

VOICES
HEARING GOD
IN A WORLD OF
IMPOSTORS

Old Testament

---

4 *"From the wilderness and this Lebanon, even as far as the great river, the river Euphrates, all the land of the Hittites, and as far as the Great Sea toward the setting of the sun will be your territory.*

5 *"No man will be able to stand before you all the days of your life. Just as I have been with Moses, I will be with you; I will not fail you or forsake you.*

6 *"Be strong and courageous, for you shall give this people possession of the land which I swore to their fathers to give them.*

7 *"Only be strong and very courageous; be careful to do according to all the law which Moses My servant commanded you; do not turn from it to the right or to the left, so that you may have success wherever you go.*

8 *"This book of the law shall not depart from your mouth, but you shall meditate on it day and night, so that you may be careful to do according to all that is written in it; for then you will make your way prosperous, and then you will have success.*

9 *"Have I not commanded you? Be strong and courageous! Do not tremble or be dismayed, for the LORD your God is with you wherever you go."*

DISCUSS with your GROUP or PONDER on your own . . .

Briefly recount Joshua's situation. What does God promise him? How is he to live? What must he do?

What written commands does God reference? What role are they to play in Joshua's life? What specifically is Joshua to do with the book of the law?

Do you meditate on God's Word day and night? How do you think this practice would change you?

ONE STEP FURTHER:

Word Study: Meditate
If you have some extra time this week, find the Hebrew word that translates "meditate" and see how it is used elsewhere in the Old Testament. If you have access to word study tools, see what they have to say also (www.blueletterbible.org is a great online tool that is easy to use!). Then, record below what biblical meditation is and how you can incorporate it into your life.

VOICES
HEARING GOD
IN A WORLD OF
IMPOSTORS

Week Four: **From Hearing to Deafness**

ACTIONS THAT SPEAK LOUDER THAN WORDS

After 40 years of wandering in the wilderness, the people of God send two spies to enter Jericho to see God's Word to Abraham, Isaac, and Jacob being fulfilled—the land of Canaan being given to the sons of Israel. The spies meet Rahab who confirms that the people of the land heard about the God who defeated Pharaoh and because of this their hearts were melting in fear. While God had been communicating face-to-face with Moses, His actions on Israel's behalf in Egypt were "speaking" loudly to the nations.

God again speaks to Joshua as he and the people camp on the plains of Moab (east of the Jordan River) preparing to enter the Promised Land. Let's take a look.

OBSERVE the TEXT of SCRIPTURE

READ Joshua 3:7-13. **MARK** every occurrence of *know.*

Joshua 3:7-13

7 *Now the LORD said to Joshua, "This day I will begin to exalt you in the sight of all Israel, that they may know that just as I have been with Moses, I will be with you.*

8 *"You shall, moreover, command the priests who are carrying the ark of the covenant, saying, 'When you come to the edge of the waters of the Jordan, you shall stand still in the Jordan.'"*

9 *Then Joshua said to the sons of Israel, "Come here, and hear the words of the LORD your God."*

10 *Joshua said, "By this you shall know that the living God is among you, and that He will assuredly dispossess from before you the Canaanite, the Hittite, the Hivite, the Perizzite, the Girgashite, the Amorite, and the Jebusite.*

11 *"Behold, the ark of the covenant of the Lord of all the earth is crossing over ahead of you into the Jordan.*

12 *"Now then, take for yourselves twelve men from the tribes of Israel, one man for each tribe.*

13 *"It shall come about when the soles of the feet of the priests who carry the ark of the LORD, the Lord of all the earth, rest in the waters of the Jordan, the waters of the Jordan will be cut off, and the waters which are flowing down from above will stand in one heap."*

DISCUSS with your GROUP or PONDER on your own . . .

Why does the LORD say He will begin to exalt Joshua in the sight of the people?

How did Israel know that her leaders were from God? How do we know it today?

Do you assume everyone in a position of church leadership is from God? Why/why not? How can you discern this today?

Digging Deeper

Voices in Joshua's Life

Moses' influence undoubtedly shaped Joshua's thinking over the years they spent together in God's service. After Moses' death, God spoke to Joshua but His was not the only voice in his life. If you have some extra time this week, consider some of the passages we haven't looked at and see what you can discover about the voices Joshua listened to and the outcomes they led to.

On what other occasions did God speak to Joshua? What prompted the interactions? What were the outcomes?

On what occasions did Joshua listen to the voice of people (Israelites or others) and get bad results?

What can you learn about listening to the voice of people from Joshua?

ONE STEP FURTHER:

Searching a Phrase

For the most part, when we do a word study we're looking for a particular word in the original language. We find the English word in a particular verse and then we use a concordance to locate the Strong's number that will take us to the original Hebrew or Greek word and we see where else and how else the word is used in Scripture.

From time to time, searching on a phrase in English can help us find what we're looking for. For example, to find out what "face to face" means we would have to wade through 2,127 occurrences of the Hebrew root *panim* ("face") because it is so common. If, though, we search on the phrase "face to face" (enclose the phrase in quotation marks) we narrow our results substantially.

If you have time this week, search on "face to face" and see what you can find out about who talked "face to face" and what "face to face" means. Record your findings below.

VOICES
Hearing God
in a World of
Impostors

Old Testament

ALL THE WORDS FOR ALL THE PEOPLE

Israel enters the Promised Land with a stunning victory at Jericho. On the heels of the victory, though, they sustain an unexpected loss—their being driven away from the small town of Ai as a result of sin in their camp. After Israel purges the sin, God gives Joshua clear and specific instructions for defeating Ai. Then, in the wake of the victory, Joshua reads the Word of God to the people.

OBSERVE the TEXT of SCRIPTURE

READ Joshua 8:30-35. **MARK** every reference to *wrote/written*, *words/law*, and *all*.

Joshua 8:30-35

30 *Then Joshua built an altar to the LORD, the God of Israel, in Mount Ebal,*

31 *just as Moses the servant of the LORD had commanded the sons of Israel, as it is written in the book of the law of Moses, an altar of uncut stones on which no man had wielded an iron tool; and they offered burnt offerings on it to the LORD, and sacrificed peace offerings.*

32 *He wrote there on the stones a copy of the law of Moses, which he had written, in the presence of the sons of Israel.*

33 *All Israel with their elders and officers and their judges were standing on both sides of the ark before the Levitical priests who carried the ark of the covenant of the LORD, the stranger as well as the native. Half of them stood in front of Mount Gerizim and half of them in front of Mount Ebal, just as Moses the servant of the LORD had given command at first to bless the people of Israel.*

34 *Then afterward he read all the words of the law, the blessing and the curse, according to all that is written in the book of the law.*

35 *There was not a word of all that Moses had commanded which Joshua did not read before all the assembly of Israel with the women and the little ones and the strangers who were living among them.*

DISCUSS with your GROUP or PONDER on your own . . .

What does Joshua construct in Mount Ebal? Why? What does he write there?

What does Joshua read? How much? How are the people involved? How many of them participate? Again, how specific were the Words God had given to Moses?

ONE STEP FURTHER:

The Case of Achan

If you have some extra time this week, see if you can find out how God revealed that Achan was the man who had taken items "under the ban." His story is in Joshua 7. Record your observations below.

Do we pay attention to all the Words of God? Where do we fall short? Do we impart God's Word to all the people among us? How can you improve in your area of influence?

What kind of problems do people run into when they follow God only on the basis of what other people tell without knowing truth for themselves?

Digging Deeper

Lying Human Voices

If you have some extra time this week, read the account of the Gibeonites in Joshua 9 and 10. When all seems to be well again in the state of Israel, the Gibeonites stroll onto the scene and dupe Joshua with a story that sounds too good to be true . . .

Briefly summarize the Gibeonite's deception. How did they act "craftily"? What truths did they tell? What lies?

Were the Gibeonites well-intentioned? Explain your answer from the text.

What had the Israelites clearly been told not to do? Did Joshua make an honest mistake? Was there any reason for him to make a covenant? What reasons were there for him not to make a covenant?

How can truth guard us from well-intentioned lies and liars?

ONE STEP FURTHER:

Word Study: Memorial/ Remember

Throughout the Word we find God's repeated call to His people to "remember" His mighty acts. In Joshua 4:7 the people are directed to gather stones from the Jordan riverbed and set them up as a memorial, a remembrance, of God's provision of stopping the waters when they crossed the river. If you have some time this week, look up the Hebrew words for "memorial" (*zikkaron*) and "remember" (*zakar*) and see where else and how else they are used in the Old Testament. Then consider how looking back and remembering God's faithfulness in the past affects how we live going forward into the future.

JOSHUA'S CHARGE TO BE IN THE BOOK

Much of the second half of the book of Joshua is devoted to the division of the land. This people who have been living together without regard to tribe for the past 470 years will now begin separating by tribe throughout the Promised Land. They have seen with their own eyes the mighty acts of God and Joshua, now old and close to death, charges them with these words.

OBSERVE the TEXT of SCRIPTURE

READ Joshua 23:6-16. **MARK** every reference to *written/word/covenant* and to *cling*.

Joshua 23:6-16

6 *"Be very firm, then, to keep and do all that is written in the book of the law of Moses, so that you may not turn aside from it to the right hand or to the left,*

7 *so that you will not associate with these nations, these which remain among you, or mention the name of their gods, or make anyone swear by them, or serve them, or bow down to them.*

8 *"But you are to cling to the LORD your God, as you have done to this day.*

9 *"For the LORD has driven out great and strong nations from before you; and as for you, no man has stood before you to this day.*

10 *"One of your men puts to flight a thousand, for the LORD your God is He who fights for you, just as He promised you.*

11 *"So take diligent heed to yourselves to love the LORD your God.*

12 *"For if you ever go back and cling to the rest of these nations, these which remain among you, and intermarry with them, so that you associate with them and they with you,*

13 *know with certainty that the LORD your God will not continue to drive these nations out from before you; but they will be a snare and a trap to you, and a whip on your sides and thorns in your eyes, until you perish from off this good land which the LORD your God has given you.*

14 *"Now behold, today I am going the way of all the earth, and you know in all your hearts and in all your souls that not one word of all the good words which the LORD your God spoke concerning you has failed; all have been fulfilled for you, not one of them has failed.*

15 *"It shall come about that just as all the good words which the LORD your God spoke to you have come upon you, so the LORD will bring upon you all the threats, until He has destroyed you from off this good land which the LORD your God has given you.*

16 *"When you transgress the covenant of the LORD your God, which He commanded you, and go and serve other gods and bow down to them, then the anger of the LORD will burn against you, and you will perish quickly from off the good land which He has given you."*

ONE STEP FURTHER:

Dividing the Land
How did God make known *who* should have *what* land? If you have some time this week, look into Joshua 18 to find out. Then record what you learned below.

VOICES
HEARING GOD
IN A WORLD OF
IMPOSTORS

DISCUSS with your GROUP or PONDER on your own . . .

What does Joshua instruct the people to do with regard to the law? What does this presuppose?

FYI:

Casting Lots
The lot is cast into the lap,
But its every decision is from the LORD.
—Proverbs 16:33

What will loving and clinging to the LORD involve for them? How do we love and cling to God today? Explain.

Why can the people trust "the good words" (Joshua 23:15) of God? What can they trust about the word of God if they disobey?

Why was it so important that they know and follow God's written and revealed Word? What will happen if they don't?

What happens today when people stray from God's revealed Word in Scripture?

VOICES
HEARING GOD
IN A WORLD OF
IMPOSTORS

WHAT COULD POSSIBLY GO WRONG?

God gave His people a clear, written Word—commands on how to live in the Promised Land they were inheriting. Unlike previous generations, they were no longer exclusively dependent on visions or prophets or signs. God had given these people not only the Promised Land but also a written Word. Under such perfect conditions, what could possibly go wrong?

The Time of the Judges

After Joshua and his generation died, a generation arose that did not know the LORD or the works He had done for Israel. For 350 years, God raised up judges to lead His people out of oppression until they rejected God and demanded a king like the other nations had. God gave them Saul, anointed by Samuel the last judge. The time of the judges in Israel is recorded in the books of Judges and Ruth. As we'll see later in this lesson, word from the Lord was rare in the time of the judges, but God had given His written word to His people. They had the Book and yet most did not follow or obey. Let's take a look.

OBSERVE the TEXT of SCRIPTURE

READ Judges 2:1-12 **MARK** every reference to *the angel of the LORD* including pronouns.

Judges 2:1-12

1 Now the angel of the LORD came up from Gilgal to Bochim. And he said, "I brought you up out of Egypt and led you into the land which I have sworn to your fathers; and I said, 'I will never break My covenant with you,

2 and as for you, you shall make no covenant with the inhabitants of this land; you shall tear down their altars.' But you have not obeyed Me; what is this you have done?

3 "Therefore I also said, 'I will not drive them out before you; but they will become as thorns in your sides and their gods will be a snare to you.' "

4 When the angel of the LORD spoke these words to all the sons of Israel, the people lifted up their voices and wept.

5 So they named that place Bochim; and there they sacrificed to the LORD.

6 When Joshua had dismissed the people, the sons of Israel went each to his inheritance to possess the land.

7 The people served the LORD all the days of Joshua, and all the days of the elders who survived Joshua, who had seen all the great work of the LORD which He had done for Israel.

8 Then Joshua the son of Nun, the servant of the LORD, died at the age of one hundred and ten.

9 And they buried him in the territory of his inheritance in Timnath-heres, in the hill country of Ephraim, north of Mount Gaash.

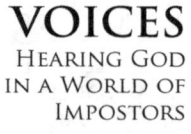

10   All that generation also were gathered to their fathers; and there arose another generation after them who did not know the LORD, nor yet the work which He had done for Israel.

11   Then the sons of Israel did evil in the sight of the LORD and served the Baals,

12   and they forsook the LORD, the God of their fathers, who had brought them out of the land of Egypt, and followed other gods from among the gods of the peoples who were around them, and bowed themselves down to them; thus they provoked the LORD to anger.

DISCUSS with your GROUP or PONDER on your own . . .

What message does the angel of the LORD bring to the people?

How well have the people done with the revealed Word of God so far? What specific and clear commands have they violated? What results will breaking God's covenant bring?

Describe the generations that lived under the rule of the judges and compare them to your generation. Was God's requirement clear to them? Is it clear today? Explain your reasoning from the text.

Why didn't they know God? How could they have known God? (Check out Deuteronomy 6 as you answer.)

Did the people of Israel need to see miracles firsthand? Do we? Explain. (As you answer, consider what Jesus said about a generation that seeks signs in Matthew 16:4.)

ONE STEP FURTHER:

Teach, Talk, Bind, Write

If you have a little margin this week, spend some time in Deuteronomy 6. What instructions did Moses give the people with regard to themselves? With regard to their children? According to Deuteronomy 6, what difference could obedience have made in the national life of Israel? What difference can it make in your life and your family's life today? Record your observations and thoughts below.

VOICES

HEARING GOD
IN A WORLD OF
IMPOSTORS

Old Testament

MESSAGES FOR DEBORAH, GIDEON, AND SAMSON'S PARENTS

Although God's people largely ignore His Word during the time of the judges, He still delivers them from foreign oppressors when they call to Him. In this process, God communicates with four individuals: Deborah, Gideon, and Samson's parents. Let's look at and compare their experiences.

OBSERVE the TEXT of SCRIPTURE

READ the account of Deborah in Judges 4, Gideon in Judges 6–7, and Samson's parents in Judges 13.

DISCUSS with your GROUP or PONDER on your own . . .

Describe each person who receives a message from God. Who are they? What are they up to when they receive it? Are they actively looking for a message from God or are they up to something else?

Deborah

Gideon

Samson's parents

Similarities/Differences:

ONE STEP FURTHER:

More Hard Words

If you have time, check out the hard words God gives to the people in Judges 6:7-10 and 10:11-14. Our culture often romanticizes the idea of "hearing from God" but biblically speaking a word from the Lord did not always mean things were going well. Just wait until we get to the prophets!

Explain (if the text says) *how* the message is delivered to each person. How does each respond? How does God meet each of them where they are?

Deborah

Gideon

Samson's parents

Similarities/Differences:

Are the messages clear? Record the specifics of each message then tell what happens. How is each authenticated? What is the big-picture outcome of each message?

Deborah

Gideon

Week Four: **From Hearing to Deafness**

Samson's parents

Similarities/Differences:

ONE STEP FURTHER:

A Midianite's Dream

In Judges 7:6-15 God calms Gideon's fears by letting him overhear a Midianite recounting a dream and a second Midianite interpreting it. If you have some extra time this week, look a little more closely at the account and without concluding things that are not in the text, consider God's sovereignty in this situation. Then record your observations and thoughts below.

Is anything commanded in these texts that we are to follow today? Are there any prescribed behaviors? Explain your thinking.

Deborah

Gideon

Samson's parents

Similarities/Differences:

WHEN EARS BECOME DULL

Poor Micah. He lived during a time when a word from the Lord was becoming rare. He was not like Moses or Joshua or even like Samson's parents. He had no *new* word from God but he had the clear *old* ones to make his way with, as we'll soon see. Let's look at his story. Read it through first in your Bible, then we'll look at it together and consider Micah's actions against some very basic truths God had already written down.

OBSERVE the TEXT of SCRIPTURE

READ Judges 17 in your Bible. Then, read through the text below and **MARK** every reference to *image* and *idol*.

Judges 17

1 Now there was a man of the hill country of Ephraim whose name was Micah.

2 He said to his mother, "The eleven hundred pieces of silver which were taken from you, about which you uttered a curse in my hearing, behold, the silver is with me; I took it." And his mother said, "Blessed be my son by the LORD."

> **But God already said . . .**
>
> **Exodus 20:12**
>
> 12 "Honor your father and your mother, that your days may be prolonged in the land which the LORD your God gives you.
>
> **Exodus 20:15**
>
> 15 You shall not steal.
>
> **Leviticus 19:11**
>
> 11 You shall not steal, nor deal falsely, nor lie to one another.

3 He then returned the eleven hundred pieces of silver to his mother, and his mother said, "I wholly dedicate the silver from my hand to the LORD for my son to make a graven image and a molten image; now therefore, I will return them to you."

4 So when he returned the silver to his mother, his mother took two hundred pieces of silver and gave them to the silversmith who made them into a graven image and a molten image, and they were in the house of Micah.

> **But God already said . . .**
>
> **Exodus 20:4**
>
> 4 "You shall not make for yourself an idol, or any likeness of what is in heaven above or on the earth beneath or in the water under the earth.
>
> **Exodus 34:17**
>
> 7 "You shall make for yourself no molten gods.

FYI:

A Pretty Big Heist

Micah stole 1,100 pieces of silver but this means little without context. Judges 16:5 gives us something for comparison when it tells us that five lords of the Philistines agreed to kick in 1,100 each as payment to Delilah for her help in subduing Samson.

5 *And the man Micah had a shrine and he made an ephod and household idols and consecrated one of his sons, that he might become his priest.*

But God already said . . .

Exodus 40:13-16

13 *"You shall put the holy garments on Aaron and anoint him and consecrate him, that he may minister as a priest to Me.*

14 *"You shall bring his sons and put tunics on them;*

15 *and you shall anoint them even as you have anointed their father, that they may minister as priests to Me; and their anointing will qualify them for a perpetual priesthood throughout their generations."*

16 *Thus Moses did; according to all that the LORD had commanded him, so he did.*

---

6 *In those days there was no king in Israel; every man did what was right in his own eyes.*

7 *Now there was a young man from Bethlehem in Judah, of the family of Judah, who was a Levite; and he was staying there.*

8 *Then the man departed from the city, from Bethlehem in Judah, to stay wherever he might find a place; and as he made his journey, he came to the hill country of Ephraim to the house of Micah.*

9 *Micah said to him, "Where do you come from?" And he said to him, "I am a Levite from Bethlehem in Judah, and I am going to stay wherever I may find a place."*

10 *Micah then said to him, "Dwell with me and be a father and a priest to me, and I will give you ten pieces of silver a year, a suit of clothes, and your maintenance." So the Levite went in.*

11 *The Levite agreed to live with the man, and the young man became to him like one of his sons.*

12 *So Micah consecrated the Levite, and the young man became his priest and lived in the house of Micah.*

13 *Then Micah said, "Now I know that the LORD will prosper me, seeing I have a Levite as priest."*

But God already said . . .

Deuteronomy 12:5

5 *"But you shall seek the LORD at the place which the LORD your God will choose from all your tribes, to establish His name there for His dwelling, and there you shall come.*

DISCUSS with your GROUP or PONDER on your own . . .

What bad behaviors in verses 1-5 could have been rationalized or misconstrued as "good" in some sense? Explain how.

How does Micah's offense against his mother compare with God's recorded words in Exodus and Leviticus? Is there any clue as to why he confessed?

Should either Micah or Mom have thought making an image was a good idea? What clear written instructions had God given on that one?

What was wrong with making a family member a priest?

What about setting up his own little "chapel"? Should Micah have known better? Why?

VOICES
HEARING GOD
IN A WORLD OF
IMPOSTORS

Old Testament

97

Week Four: **From Hearing to Deafness**

Did Micah have adequate information to obey God God's way? Did his craving for "something more" benefit him in any way? Explain.

What type of "religious" or "spiritual" behaviors do people rationalize today that are not plumb when held up to God's revealed Word?

God communicates with people throughout the book of Judges with the intent of delivering them from bondage. The bondage, of course, has come as a result of them not remembering the words and acts of God and aligning their lives with His clear and now written words and statutes. When this happens, all kinds of weird strains of "spirituality" start growing. Micah of Ephraim gives us a glimpse of man's condition when he's lost the plumb line. As we keep reading, it gets worse.

OBSERVE the TEXT of SCRIPTURE

READ Judges 18:1-6. **MARK** every reference to God (God, LORD).

Judges 18:1-6

1   In those days there was no king of Israel; and in those days the tribe of the Danites was seeking an inheritance for themselves to live in, for until that day an inheritance had not been allotted to them as a possession among the tribes of Israel.

2   So the sons of Dan sent from their family five men out of their whole number, valiant men from Zorah and Eshtaol, to spy out the land and to search it; and they said to them, "Go, search the land." And they came to the hill country of Ephraim, to the house of Micah, and lodged there.

3   When they were near the house of Micah, they recognized the voice of the young man, the Levite; and they turned aside there and said to him, "Who brought you here? And what are you doing in this place? And what do you have here?"

4   He said to them, "Thus and so has Micah done to me, and he has hired me and I have become his priest."

5   They said to him, "Inquire of God, please, that we may know whether our way on which we are going will be prosperous."

6   The priest said to them, "Go in peace; your way in which you are going has the LORD'S approval."

DISCUSS with your GROUP or PONDER on your own . . .

When the sons of Dan find out that the young Levite is acting as a priest for Micah, how do they respond? Based on God's revealed Word, what was the right response?

Based on Scripture, do you think this young Levite had God's approval? Why/why not?

Could this Levite truly "inquire of God"? Explain. How could the Danites have known the difference?

If you were one of the Danites, would you have accepted the Levite's approval as from God? Explain.

Does a person's claim to speak on behalf of God make it so? How could the Danites have measured this voice? Against what? How can we measure similar voices today?

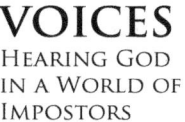

VOICES
HEARING GOD
IN A WORLD OF
IMPOSTORS

Week Four: **From Hearing to Deafness**

@THE END OF THE DAY . . .

Next week we'll head to the time of the kings of Israel as we continue to see how God spoke to the fathers in the prophets. For now, spend some time considering what your biggest take away from your time in the Word this week has been and summarize it in no more than a couple of sentences.

WEEK FIVE

Hard Words from a Sovereign God

*. . . word from the LORD was rare in those days,
visions were infrequent.*
—1 Samuel 3:1

A new word from the LORD was rare during the period of the judges but Israel had written words . . . words they consistently ignored and rejected. When the period of the judges ended God spoke again, this time to a little boy named Samuel. If you've never actually studied this account, it's tempting to think "Oh, how sweet, God talked to a little boy!" The words to the boy, however, were words of judgment against a priest and his sons who had ignored God's written Word. In the days that followed God revealed Himself not only to Samuel but also to each of the first three kings of Israel—Saul, David, and Solomon.

Week Five: **Hard Words from a Sovereign God**

"SPEAK, LORD, FOR YOUR SERVANT IS LISTENING"

Samuel, the last judge of Israel, anointed the nation's first two kings. Born to a previously barren mother, he grew up serving in the tabernacle of God at Shiloh. Before God sends a message to Eli through Samuel, He sends Eli a message through an unnamed "man of God."

OBSERVE the TEXT of SCRIPTURE

READ the account of the man of God and Eli in 1 Samuel 2:27-36

DISCUSS with your GROUP or PONDER on your own . . .

Who brings God's Word to Eli? Are we told specifically how it happened?

What does God accuse Eli of doing? What will be the result of his actions? How will Eli know the word is reliable?

Is this the kind of "word from God" people seek today? Explain.

OBSERVE the TEXT of SCRIPTURE

READ 1 Samuel 3. **MARK** every reference to *called* and *listening*.

1 Samuel 3:1-15

1   *Now the boy Samuel was ministering to the LORD before Eli. And word from the LORD was rare in those days, visions were infrequent.*

2   *It happened at that time as Eli was lying down in his place (now his eyesight had begun to grow dim and he could not see well),*

3   *and the lamp of God had not yet gone out, and Samuel was lying down in the temple of the LORD where the ark of God was,*

4   *that the LORD called Samuel; and he said, "Here I am."*

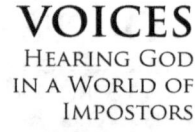

5   Then he ran to Eli and said, "Here I am, for you called me." But he said, "I did not call, lie down again." So he went and lay down.

6   The LORD called yet again, "Samuel!" So Samuel arose and went to Eli and said, "Here I am, for you called me." But he answered, "I did not call, my son, lie down again."

7   Now Samuel did not yet know the LORD, nor had the word of the LORD yet been revealed to him.

8   So the LORD called Samuel again for the third time. And he arose and went to Eli and said, "Here I am, for you called me." Then Eli discerned that the LORD was calling the boy.

9   And Eli said to Samuel, "Go lie down, and it shall be if He calls you, that you shall say, 'Speak, LORD, for Your servant is listening.' " So Samuel went and lay down in his place.

10   Then the LORD came and stood and called as at other times, "Samuel! Samuel!" And Samuel said, "Speak, for Your servant is listening."

11   The LORD said to Samuel, "Behold, I am about to do a thing in Israel at which both ears of everyone who hears it will tingle.

12   "In that day I will carry out against Eli all that I have spoken concerning his house, from beginning to end.

13   "For I have told him that I am about to judge his house forever for the iniquity which he knew, because his sons brought a curse on themselves and he did not rebuke them.

14   "Therefore I have sworn to the house of Eli that the iniquity of Eli's house shall not be atoned for by sacrifice or offering forever."

15   So Samuel lay down until morning. Then he opened the doors of the house of the LORD. But Samuel was afraid to tell the vision to Eli.

DISCUSS with your GROUP or PONDER on your own . . .

Describe the times. Specifically, what does the text say about the frequency of words and visions from God?

Describe Samuel and his situation.

ONE STEP FURTHER:

Word Study: Listen

If you have extra time this week, find the Hebrew word that translates "listen." How common is it? How else is it interpreted throughout the Old Testament? What results do listening and not listening to God's voice bring? Record your finding below.

FYI:

Hear, O Israel . . .

While the Hebrew *shema* (hear, listen) is a high-frequency biblical word, perhaps its most recognizable appearance comes in Deuteronomy 6:4: "Hear, O Israel! The LORD is our God, the LORD is one!"

VOICES

HEARING GOD
IN A WORLD OF
IMPOSTORS

Old Testament

Week Five: **Hard Words from a Sovereign God**

What people are mentioned in this text? Which one does the LORD call? How many times does He call?

ONE STEP FURTHER:

A Clear Word to Samuel

When God calls Samuel to anoint a king, there is no ambiguity. God tells Samuel when Saul will show up, where he will come from and what he will do to the Philistines. If you have time, check it out for yourself in 1 Samuel 9:16-17 and record your observations below.

Who recognizes God's voice initially? Explain. When Samuel recognizes God's voice, what does he consistently do?

What does God tell Eli through Samuel? How would you characterize the message? Is it something you'd have wanted to hear from God? How does this tie in with the word from the man of God? With events that will come later?

FYI:

Samuel Confirmed as a True Prophet

Eli the priest received two messages from God that agreed with one another and subsequently came true—one was delivered by an unnamed "man of God," the other by young Samuel. Eli knew Samuel heard God's voice because his message confirmed the message he had already received from the man of God in 1 Samuel 2. It wasn't until the words were fulfilled, though, that the people *knew* he was confirmed as a prophet of the LORD.

GOD'S PEOPLE IGNORE GOD'S WORDS

God gives the people the king they so desperately desire and He gives the king instructions. While showing early signs of being a good king, Saul quickly disobeys specific words from God. We'll look at one instance together. Then, in our remaining time we'll focus on God's words to David and Solomon. As we pick up the story in 1 Samuel 15, Saul has already disregarded and disobeyed God's commandment and offered a sacrifice, usurping Samuel's role as priest.

VOICES
HEARING GOD
IN A WORLD OF
IMPOSTORS

104

Old Testament

Digging Deeper

God's Response to the People's Call for a King

In 1 Samuel 8 God responds to the people's cry for a king. If you have time this week, examine His interaction with Samuel and His words to the people. As you study, note specifically how God refers back to what He revealed to Moses and had him preserve in writing.

God's word to Samuel

God's word to the people

Basic rules for living with a king

Basic rules for the king

God's warning about kings

Summary

OBSERVE the TEXT of SCRIPTURE

READ 1 Samuel 15. **MARK** every reference to *word of the LORD/voice of the LORD* and to *rejected*.

1 Samuel 15

1 Then Samuel said to Saul, "The LORD sent me to anoint you as king over His people, over Israel; now therefore, listen to the words of the LORD.

2 "Thus says the LORD of hosts, 'I will punish Amalek for what he did to Israel, how he set himself against him on the way while he was coming up from Egypt.

3 'Now go and strike Amalek and utterly destroy all that he has, and do not spare him; but put to death both man and woman, child and infant, ox and sheep, camel and donkey.' "

4 Then Saul summoned the people and numbered them in Telaim, 200,000 foot soldiers and 10,000 men of Judah.

5 Saul came to the city of Amalek and set an ambush in the valley.

VOICES
HEARING GOD
IN A WORLD OF
IMPOSTORS

6 Saul said to the Kenites, "Go, depart, go down from among the Amalekites, so that I do not destroy you with them; for you showed kindness to all the sons of Israel when they came up from Egypt." So the Kenites departed from among the Amalekites.

7 So Saul defeated the Amalekites, from Havilah as you go to Shur, which is east of Egypt.

8 He captured Agag the king of the Amalekites alive, and utterly destroyed all the people with the edge of the sword.

9 But Saul and the people spared Agag and the best of the sheep, the oxen, the fatlings, the lambs, and all that was good, and were not willing to destroy them utterly; but everything despised and worthless, that they utterly destroyed.

10 Then the word of the LORD came to Samuel, saying,

11 "I regret that I have made Saul king, for he has turned back from following Me and has not carried out My commands." And Samuel was distressed and cried out to the LORD all night.

12 Samuel rose early in the morning to meet Saul; and it was told Samuel, saying, "Saul came to Carmel, and behold, he set up a monument for himself, then turned and proceeded on down to Gilgal."

13 Samuel came to Saul, and Saul said to him, "Blessed are you of the LORD! I have carried out the command of the LORD."

14 But Samuel said, "What then is this bleating of the sheep in my ears, and the lowing of the oxen which I hear?"

15 Saul said, "They have brought them from the Amalekites, for the people spared the best of the sheep and oxen, to sacrifice to the LORD your God; but the rest we have utterly destroyed."

16 Then Samuel said to Saul, "Wait, and let me tell you what the LORD said to me last night." And he said to him, "Speak!"

17 Samuel said, "Is it not true, though you were little in your own eyes, you were made the head of the tribes of Israel? And the LORD anointed you king over Israel,

18 and the LORD sent you on a mission, and said, 'Go and utterly destroy the sinners, the Amalekites, and fight against them until they are exterminated.'

19 "Why then did you not obey the voice of the LORD, but rushed upon the spoil and did what was evil in the sight of the LORD?"

20 Then Saul said to Samuel, "I did obey the voice of the LORD, and went on the mission on which the LORD sent me, and have brought back Agag the king of Amalek, and have utterly destroyed the Amalekites.

21 "But the people took some of the spoil, sheep and oxen, the choicest of the things devoted to destruction, to sacrifice to the LORD your God at Gilgal."

22 Samuel said,

"Has the LORD as much delight in burnt offerings and sacrifices

As in obeying the voice of the LORD?

Behold, to obey is better than sacrifice,

And to heed than the fat of rams.

23 "For rebellion is as the sin of divination,

And insubordination is as iniquity and idolatry.

Because you have rejected the word of the LORD,

He has also rejected you from being king."

24 Then Saul said to Samuel, "I have sinned; I have indeed transgressed the command of the LORD and your words, because I feared the people and listened to their voice.

25 "Now therefore, please pardon my sin and return with me, that I may worship the LORD."

26 But Samuel said to Saul, "I will not return with you; for you have rejected the word of the LORD, and the LORD has rejected you from being king over Israel."

27 As Samuel turned to go, Saul seized the edge of his robe, and it tore.

28 So Samuel said to him, "The LORD has torn the kingdom of Israel from you today and has given it to your neighbor, who is better than you.

29 "Also the Glory of Israel will not lie or change His mind; for He is not a man that He should change His mind."

30 Then he said, "I have sinned; but please honor me now before the elders of my people and before Israel, and go back with me, that I may worship the LORD your God."

31 So Samuel went back following Saul, and Saul worshiped the LORD.

32 Then Samuel said, "Bring me Agag, the king of the Amalekites." And Agag came to him cheerfully. And Agag said, "Surely the bitterness of death is past."

33 But Samuel said, "As your sword has made women childless, so shall your mother be childless among women." And Samuel hewed Agag to pieces before the LORD at Gilgal.

34 Then Samuel went to Ramah, but Saul went up to his house at Gibeah of Saul.

35 Samuel did not see Saul again until the day of his death; for Samuel grieved over Saul. And the LORD regretted that He had made Saul king over Israel.

DISCUSS with your GROUP or PONDER on your own . . .

What does the LORD tell Saul through Samuel? What does He specifically command him to do? To not do? Is He clear?

ONE STEP FURTHER:

"Whose hearts God had touched . . ."

In 1 Samuel 10:26 God moves men to action. The text says that when Saul went back to Gibeah "valiant *men* whose hearts God touched went with him." If you have some extra time this week, find the Hebrew word that translates "touch" and see how else it is used throughout the Old Testament. Where else is it used of God? Is it typically positive or negative? Summarize your findings.

FYI:

Remember the Word to Joshua

If Saul had been reading the Book, he'd have known that God was deadly serious about Amalek. The first thing God asked Moses to write down was a word for Joshua about the Amalekites. Remember Exodus 17:14-16? "Then the LORD said to Moses, "Write this in a book as a memorial and recite it to Joshua, that I will utterly blot out the memory of Amalek from under heaven." Moses built an altar and named it The LORD is My Banner; and he said, "The LORD has sworn; the LORD will have war against Amalek from generation to generation."

VOICES
HEARING GOD
IN A WORLD OF
IMPOSTORS

How does Saul respond? What does he do/not do? How do his actions measure up to God's commands? Explain.

ONE STEP FURTHER:

Dreams or Urim or Prophets

We've seen examples of God speaking in dreams and through prophets. This week, see what you can discover about "Urim." Record your findings below.

What does the LORD say to Samuel in response to Saul's actions? How does God characterize Saul's behavior? By contrast, how does Saul characterize his own behavior?

What message from God does Samuel give Saul after the battle? What is the heart of the problem? How does Saul react to God's Word to him?

How does Samuel characterize Saul's response to God's Word in verse 23? What will happen to him in turn?

What voice had Saul chosen? In what ways do people reject the Word of God today? In what situations are you most tempted to do this? How can we guard against elevating man's words and our own feelings above the Word of God?

CONSEQUENCES OF REJECTING GOD'S WORD

It's not long before God tells Samuel to anoint David as the next king. David, however, does not ascend to the throne immediately. Saul remains king but grows increasingly paranoid, eventually chasing David all over the land with murderous intent. By the end of his life, having repeatedly rejected God's voice and God no longer responding to him, Saul and Saul seeks other voices. The events in the following text take place as the Philistines once again threaten Israel and God refuses to answer Saul's requests for counsel.

OBSERVE the TEXT of SCRIPTURE

READ 1 Samuel 28:6-7. **MARK** every form of the word *inquire.*

1 Samuel 28:6-7

6 *When Saul inquired of the LORD, the LORD did not answer him, either by dreams or by Urim or by prophets.*

7 *Then Saul said to his servants, "Seek for me a woman who is a medium, that I may go to her and inquire of her." And his servants said to him, "Behold, there is a woman who is a medium at En-dor."*

DISCUSS with your GROUP or PONDER on your own . . .

According to the text, what were acceptable means for Saul to seek God for answers? Record some examples that you remember from what you've studied so far.

When God ceases to respond to Saul, where does he turn? Is this a continued rejection of God's revealed Word? If so, how?

Where do people turn today when seeking more than God has revealed in His Word?

ONE STEP FURTHER:

Mediums and Spiritists

If you have some extra time this week, check out where mediums and spiritists show up in the Bible. Where are they? Who consults them? What happens? Record your findings below.

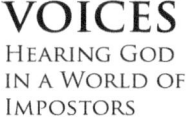

VOICES
HEARING GOD
IN A WORLD OF
IMPOSTORS

Old Testament

109

SEEKING TRUTH THROUGH FORBIDDEN MEANS

When God stopped responding to the hard-hearted king, Saul attempted to seek counsel by means which God had expressly forbidden. As you read the next section, focus on what is clear. The "difficult" section of the text (which we'll address in the sidebar) does not alter how we interpret and apply the clear words of God.

OBSERVE the TEXT of SCRIPTURE

READ 1 Samuel 28:8-19. **MARK** every form of the word *inquire*.

1 Samuel 28:8-19

8 Then Saul disguised himself by putting on other clothes, and went, he and two men with him, and they came to the woman by night; and he said, "Conjure up for me, please, and bring up for me whom I shall name to you."

9 But the woman said to him, "Behold, you know what Saul has done, how he has cut off those who are mediums and spiritists from the land. Why are you then laying a snare for my life to bring about my death?"

10 Saul vowed to her by the LORD, saying, "As the LORD lives, no punishment shall come upon you for this thing."

11 Then the woman said, "Whom shall I bring up for you?" And he said, "Bring up Samuel for me."

12 When the woman saw Samuel, she cried out with a loud voice; and the woman spoke to Saul, saying, "Why have you deceived me? For you are Saul."

13 The king said to her, "Do not be afraid; but what do you see?" And the woman said to Saul, "I see a divine being coming up out of the earth."

14 He said to her, "What is his form?" And she said, "An old man is coming up, and he is wrapped with a robe." And Saul knew that it was Samuel, and he bowed with his face to the ground and did homage.

15 Then Samuel said to Saul, "Why have you disturbed me by bringing me up?" And Saul answered, "I am greatly distressed; for the Philistines are waging war against me, and God has departed from me and no longer answers me, either through prophets or by dreams; therefore I have called you, that you may make known to me what I should do."

16 Samuel said, "Why then do you ask me, since the LORD has departed from you and has become your adversary?

17 "The LORD has done accordingly as He spoke through me; for the LORD has torn the kingdom out of your hand and given it to your neighbor, to David.

18 "As you did not obey the LORD and did not execute His fierce wrath on Amalek, so the LORD has done this thing to you this day.

19 "Moreover the LORD will also give over Israel along with you into the hands of the Philistines, therefore tomorrow you and your sons will be with me. Indeed the LORD will give over the army of Israel into the hands of the Philistines!"

FYI:

Possible "Samuels"

While the Law prohibited necromancy (Lev. 20:17; Deut. 18:11), Saul requested a medium to "call up Samuel" for him. Although the text clearly and repeatedly says Samuel appeared, students have attempted to explain this appearance several ways. Here are the most prominent:

1. The "medium" deceived Saul into thinking Samuel was there.

2. Either the Lord or the medium conjured up a demon to impersonate Samuel.

3. The medium conjured up Samuel.

4. God miraculously raised Samuel out of sheol (1 Samuel 2:6).

FYI:

Mediums

As for the person who turns to mediums and to spiritists, to play the harlot after them, I will also set My face against that person and will cut him off from among his people.

—Leviticus 20:6

DISCUSS with your GROUP or PONDER on your own . . .

In verse 15, how does Saul describe his predicament to Samuel? Why is he appealing to necromancy? What is his burning question?

Does Samuel answer his question? What message does he give Saul? What had Saul previously done with clear instructions from God?

Does Saul's disobedient pursuit of knowledge gain him anything of benefit?

How does Saul rationalize his sin? Do people today rationalize and even elevate similar sins? If so, how?

THE MAN AFTER GOD'S OWN HEART

It's easy to assume that since David was described as a man after God's own heart (1 Samuel 13:14) and since God led David throughout his life that there must have been many instances of God talking directly to David. Scripture, though, shows that overwhelmingly God communicated to David through His revealed Word and through Samuel and other prophets. He also inspired David to write many of the psalms. Let's look at the text to see David's view of God's written Word.

FYI:

A Summary of Saul's Demise

But Samuel said to Saul, "I will not return with you; for you have rejected the word of the LORD, and the LORD has rejected you from being king over Israel."

—1 Samuel 15:26

ONE STEP FURTHER:

God Was With Him

Even before David became king, people realized God was with him and was prospering him. If you have some time this week, see if you can compile a list of all the people who acknowledged that God was with David and how they knew. Record your findings below.

VOICES
HEARING GOD
IN A WORLD OF
IMPOSTORS

Old Testament

Week Five: **Hard Words from a Sovereign God**

OBSERVE the TEXT of SCRIPTURE

READ Psalm 19. **MARK** every reference to *speech* including synonyms (*voice, utterances,* etc.). Then, **MARK** references to the written word of God: *law, testimony, precepts, commandment, judgments.*

Psalm 19

For the choir director. A Psalm of David.

1 *The heavens are telling of the glory of God;*

   And their expanse is declaring the work of His hands.

2 *Day to day pours forth speech,*

   And night to night reveals knowledge.

3 *There is no speech, nor are there words;*

   Their voice is not heard.

4 *Their line has gone out through all the earth,*

   And their utterances to the end of the world.

   In them He has placed a tent for the sun,

5 *Which is as a bridegroom coming out of his chamber;*

   It rejoices as a strong man to run his course.

6 *Its rising is from one end of the heavens,*

   And its circuit to the other end of them;

   And there is nothing hidden from its heat.

7 *The law of the LORD is perfect, restoring the soul;*

   The testimony of the LORD is sure, making wise the simple.

8 *The precepts of the LORD are right, rejoicing the heart;*

   The commandment of the LORD is pure, enlightening the eyes.

9 *The fear of the LORD is clean, enduring forever;*

   The judgments of the LORD are true; they are righteous altogether.

10 *They are more desirable than gold, yes, than much fine gold;*

   Sweeter also than honey and the drippings of the honeycomb.

11 *Moreover, by them Your servant is warned;*

   In keeping them there is great reward.

12 *Who can discern his errors? Acquit me of hidden faults.*

13 *Also keep back Your servant from presumptuous sins;*

   Let them not rule over me;

   Then I will be blameless,

   And I shall be acquitted of great transgression.

14 *Let the words of my mouth and the meditation of my heart*

   Be acceptable in Your sight,

   O LORD, my rock and my Redeemer.

ONE STEP FURTHER:

Go Kill Goliath!

Did David need a specific command to take on Goliath? If you have some time this week, read the David and Goliath account in 1 Samuel 17 and note what moved David to action. Consider these questions: What did David know about the Philistines? What did he know about God? What had God proved time and again in His dealings with Israel and her enemies?

Record your observations below. Then think through implications David's example has for in your life. Do you ever ignore the clear teaching of the written Word while waiting for some "experiential word" from God before you stand *for* Him?

VOICES
HEARING GOD
IN A WORLD OF
IMPOSTORS

112

Old Testament

NOTES

DISCUSS with your GROUP or PONDER on your own . . .

In verses 1-6, what "voice" is speaking? Is it an *audible* voice? Does it have content or mood? What is it saying? What truth does it communicate?

What shift does David make in verses 7-11?

How does David describe God's written Word?

What can this written Word of God do for people? (What can it do for a relationship with God? What can it do for decision-making? What can it do for joy?)

What does David pray for in the final three verses of the psalm?

How does God's Word reveal God's will for how we live today?

FYI:

The Word Through Prophets

God used prophets to speak to David throughout his life. Samuel was the first. In the following text, Gad gives David specific and life-saving information as Saul is on the hunt . . .

"The prophet Gad said to David, "Do not stay in the stronghold; depart, and go into the land of Judah." So David departed and went into the forest of Hereth.

—1 Samuel 22:5

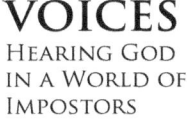

VOICES
HEARING GOD
IN A WORLD OF
IMPOSTORS

Old Testament

Digging Deeper

Other Voices in David's Life

If you have time this week, consider other voices in David's life, both good and bad, and how he accepted or rejected their words. Here are a few to get you started.

Samuel

Other Prophets

Jonathan

Abigail

His Sons

His Men

The People

ONE STEP FURTHER:

Inquiring for Keilah

If you have some time this week, study David's interactions with God in 1 Samuel 23 as he seeks to discern the next steps he should take. Note the questions he asks, the responses he receives and his men's reactions. Also note if the text tells how God answered . . . or not. Here are a few other questions to get you thinking:

When the ephod arrives, how does it affect what David does?

What does David ask God for after he has access to the ephod? Does he repeat his questions?

What action does he take?

What type of confirmation is shown in the text?

Record your observation and findings below.

VEERING FROM THE PLUMBLINE

Even hearts truly inclined toward God can encounter trouble when they veer away from revealed truth. Second Samuel 5 and 6 clearly says that God is with David and yet he hits a pothole when he begins to pursue God in a way that at surface level looks benign but was counter to what God had already revealed. Let's look for ourselves.

OBSERVE the TEXT of SCRIPTURE

READ 2 Samuel 5 and 6 and note how David is doing with reference to the written Word of God. Then, look at 2 Samuel 6:1-9 again and **MARK** every reference to *the ark.*

2 Samuel 6:1-9

1 *Now David again gathered all the chosen men of Israel, thirty thousand.*

2 *And David arose and went with all the people who were with him to Baale-judah, to bring up from there the ark of God which is called by the Name, the very name of the LORD of hosts who is enthroned above the cherubim.*

3 *They placed the ark of God on a new cart that they might bring it from the house of Abinadab which was on the hill; and Uzzah and Ahio, the sons of Abinadab, were leading the new cart.*

4 *So they brought it with the ark of God from the house of Abinadab, which was on the hill; and Ahio was walking ahead of the ark.*

5 *Meanwhile, David and all the house of Israel were celebrating before the LORD with all kinds of instruments made of fir wood, and with lyres, harps, tambourines, castanets and cymbals.*

6 *But when they came to the threshing floor of Nacon, Uzzah reached out toward the ark of God and took hold of it, for the oxen nearly upset it.*

7 *And the anger of the LORD burned against Uzzah, and God struck him down there for his irreverence; and he died there by the ark of God.*

8 *David became angry because of the LORD'S outburst against Uzzah, and that place is called Perez-uzzah to this day.*

9 *So David was afraid of the LORD that day; and he said, "How can the ark of the LORD come to me?"*

DISCUSS with your GROUP or PONDER on your own . . .

What does David accomplish in the opening verses of 2 Samuel 5:1-10? Why is he able to do such things?

ONE STEP FURTHER:

More Inquiries

If you have time this week, check out other times David "inquires of the LORD" and record what you learn.

1 Samuel 30:7-8

2 Samuel 2:1

2 Samuel 5:19-24

Does David exhibit any questionable behavior in chapter 5? (Consider specifically 2 Samuel 5:13.) If so what do you think is questionable and why? (Cite verses, not just opinions).

ONE STEP FURTHER:

Ephod

If you have some extra time this week, find the Hebrew word that translates "ephod" and see how it is used throughout the Old Testament. As you study, also watch for how it may be related to the Urim and Thummin. Ask the fives Ws and H as you study and record your findings below.

In what ways does David act well?

What does David want to do with the ark? Do you think it was a good thing that he wanted to do? From what you can observe in the text, do you think his heart was in the right place? Explain your reasoning.

What happens when he tries to move it? Does this account stir an emotional response in you? If so, what and why?

What method did David use for transport? How did this compare with the Philistines' method in 1 Samuel 6? What information should David have known that the Philistines wouldn't have?

How was the ark supposed to be transported according to God's revealed Word? (See Deut. 10:8, Num. 4:15; 7:9.)

How does David respond to the judgment initially? Does his attitude eventually align with God's revelation? Explain.

Do people today ever try to obey God in their own way and on their own terms? Is it ever based on ignorance? Was disobedience because of ignorance an acceptable excuse for David? Is it for us? Explain your answers.

Do you ever veer from God's ways like David did? If so, why do you think you do? How can you correct it?

THE BIG NEWS COMES THROUGH A PROPHET

God made a covenant with Noah speaking directly to him. He did the same with Abraham and renewed that covenant with Isaac and Jacob. God's covenant with David, though, involved a prophet. God spoke to the "man after His own heart" through a mediator. Let's take a look.

Week Five: **Hard Words from a Sovereign God**

OBSERVE the TEXT of SCRIPTURE

READ 2 Samuel 7, which records the Davidic Covenant. Then re-read 2 Samuel 7:1-6 and **MARK** distinctively every reference to *God*, *Nathan*, and *David* including pronouns.

2 Samuel 7:1-16

1 *Now it came about when the king lived in his house, and the LORD had given him rest on every side from all his enemies,*

2 *that the king said to Nathan the prophet, "See now, I dwell in a house of cedar, but the ark of God dwells within tent curtains."*

3 *Nathan said to the king, "Go, do all that is in your mind, for the LORD is with you."*

4 *But in the same night the word of the LORD came to Nathan, saying,*

5 *"Go and say to My servant David, 'Thus says the LORD, "Are you the one who should build Me a house to dwell in?*

6 *"For I have not dwelt in a house since the day I brought up the sons of Israel from Egypt, even to this day; but I have been moving about in a tent, even in a tabernacle.*

7 *"Wherever I have gone with all the sons of Israel, did I speak a word with one of the tribes of Israel, which I commanded to shepherd My people Israel, saying, 'Why have you not built Me a house of cedar?' " '*

8 *"Now therefore, thus you shall say to My servant David, 'Thus says the LORD of hosts, "I took you from the pasture, from following the sheep, to be ruler over My people Israel.*

9 *"I have been with you wherever you have gone and have cut off all your enemies from before you; and I will make you a great name, like the names of the great men who are on the earth.*

10 *"I will also appoint a place for My people Israel and will plant them, that they may live in their own place and not be disturbed again, nor will the wicked afflict them any more as formerly,*

11 *even from the day that I commanded judges to be over My people Israel; and I will give you rest from all your enemies. The LORD also declares to you that the LORD will make a house for you.*

12 *"When your days are complete and you lie down with your fathers, I will raise up your descendant after you, who will come forth from you, and I will establish his kingdom.*

13 *"He shall build a house for My name, and I will establish the throne of his kingdom forever.*

14 *"I will be a father to him and he will be a son to Me; when he commits iniquity, I will correct him with the rod of men and the strokes of the sons of men,*

15 *but My lovingkindness shall not depart from him, as I took it away from Saul, whom I removed from before you.*

16 *"Your house and your kingdom shall endure before Me forever; your throne shall be established forever." ' "*

ONE STEP FURTHER:

Famine and the Word

If you have time this week, take a look at another example of David hearing from God through His Word. In 2 Samuel 21 David seeks answers from the Lord regarding a famine in the land. On the basis of the written Word (Leviticus 26:16-20; Deuteronomy 28:16-18) he knew that a producing land was tied to obedience and that rebellion led to crop failure and famine.

If you have some extra time this week, look more closely at David's seeking after the Lord for information regarding the famine, and how God answered. As you read, be sure to pick up the original account of the Gibeonites in Joshua 9. Record your findings below.

118

VOICES
HEARING GOD
IN A WORLD OF
IMPOSTORS

Old Testament

DISCUSS with your GROUP or PONDER on your own . . .

What does David tell Nathan he wants to do? How does Nathan respond? Why?

How does God intervene? What message does He send to David through Nathan? What are the specifics of the promise?

According to the text how did Nathan hear from the LORD? Is there any indication God spoke directly to David?

How does David respond to the Word from God through the prophet?

How have you been responding to the Word from God through the prophets (Hebrews 1:1; 2 Peter 1:20-21) that we have in Scripture?

VOICES
HEARING GOD
IN A WORLD OF
IMPOSTORS

Digging Deeper

Hard Words from Nathan and Gad

Prophets brought good words to David, great words actually. Samuel told him God had chosen him to be king and Nathan brought word that God was going to build David an enduring house. Prophets, though, also spoke severe words. The same prophet who told David about the covenant God would make with him delivered words of judgment after he sinned against Bathsheba and Uriah. The prophet Gad helped David when he was on the run from Saul and told him of God's coming judgment for numbering the people. If you have some time this week, study on your own the hard words the prophets Nathan and Gad brought to David.

God's Words through Nathan (2 Samuel 12)

God's Words through Gad (2 Samuel 24)

WHOM GOD APPEARED TO TWICE . . .

While there is no biblical record of God appearing to David—the man after His own heart—1 Kings 11:9 says that God appeared to Solomon twice. You'd think that two appearances would produce a better outcome, but alas, Solomon only started well.

OBSERVE the TEXT of SCRIPTURE

READ 1 Kings 3:5-15a. **MARK** every reference to *God* including synonyms and pronouns.

1 Kings 3:5-15a

5   *In Gibeon the LORD appeared to Solomon in a dream at night; and God said, "Ask what you wish me to give you."*

6   *Then Solomon said, "You have shown great lovingkindness to Your servant David my father, according as he walked before You in truth and righteousness and uprightness of heart toward You; and You have reserved for him this great lovingkindness, that You have given him a son to sit on his throne, as it is this day.*

VOICES
HEARING GOD
IN A WORLD OF
IMPOSTORS

120

Old Testament

7   "Now, O LORD my God, You have made Your servant king in place of my father David, yet I am but a little child; I do not know how to go out or come in.

8   "Your servant is in the midst of Your people which You have chosen, a great people who are too many to be numbered or counted.

9   "So give Your servant an understanding heart to judge Your people to discern between good and evil. For who is able to judge this great people of Yours?"

10 It was pleasing in the sight of the Lord that Solomon had asked this thing.

11 God said to him, "Because you have asked this thing and have not asked for yourself long life, nor have asked riches for yourself, nor have you asked for the life of your enemies, but have asked for yourself discernment to understand justice,

12 behold, I have done according to your words. Behold, I have given you a wise and discerning heart, so that there has been no one like you before you, nor shall one like you arise after you.

13 "I have also given you what you have not asked, both riches and honor, so that there will not be any among the kings like you all your days.

14 "If you walk in My ways, keeping My statutes and commandments, as your father David walked, then I will prolong your days."

15 Then Solomon awoke, and behold, it was a dream.

Digging Deeper

The Sons Before Solomon

Solomon was heir to his father's throne, but he wasn't David's oldest son. Three of his older brothers listened to wrong voices to their destruction. If you have some time this week, look at the lives of Amnon, Absalom, and Abijah to see what voices they listened to and what happened.

Amnon

Absalom

Abijah

Week Five: **Hard Words from a Sovereign God**

DISCUSS with your GROUP or PONDER on your own . . .

How does God appear to Solomon the first time? What does He ask Solomon? How does Solomon answer? (Be careful to stick to the text.)

How does God respond? What does He tell Solomon He will do for him?

How do we know this wasn't "just a dream"? What confirms that it was more than that?

A SECOND APPEARANCE FROM GOD

David followed faithfully with his whole heart and God spoke to him primarily through His written Word and prophets. Solomon started well, asked wisely, built the temple and God appeared to him twice along the way. Let's check out the second appearance.

OBSERVE the TEXT of SCRIPTURE

READ 1 Kings 9:1-9. **MARK** every reference to God *(God, Lord)*.

1 Kings 9:1-9

1   *Now it came about when Solomon had finished building the house of the LORD, and the king's house, and all that Solomon desired to do,*

2   *that the LORD appeared to Solomon a second time, as He had appeared to him at Gibeon.*

3   *The LORD said to him, "I have heard your prayer and your supplication, which you have made before Me; I have consecrated this house which you have built by putting My name there forever, and My eyes and My heart will be there perpetually.*

4 "As for you, if you will walk before Me as your father David walked, in integrity of heart and uprightness, doing according to all that I have commanded you and will keep My statutes and My ordinances,

5 then I will establish the throne of your kingdom over Israel forever, just as I promised to your father David, saying, 'You shall not lack a man on the throne of Israel.'

6 "But if you or your sons indeed turn away from following Me, and do not keep My commandments and My statutes which I have set before you, and go and serve other gods and worship them,

7 then I will cut off Israel from the land which I have given them, and the house which I have consecrated for My name, I will cast out of My sight. So Israel will become a proverb and a byword among all peoples.

8 "And this house will become a heap of ruins; everyone who passes by will be astonished and hiss and say, 'Why has the LORD done thus to this land and to this house?'

9 "And they will say, 'Because they forsook the LORD their God, who brought their fathers out of the land of Egypt, and adopted other gods and worshiped them and served them, therefore the LORD has brought all this adversity on them.' "

DISCUSS with your GROUP or PONDER on your own . . .

When does the LORD appear to Solomon the second time? How does it compare to the first?

Summarize the LORD's Word to Solomon.

What positive and negative "if/then" statements does God make?

Week Five: **Hard Words from a Sovereign God**

What is at the heart of the if/then statements? How does God characterize the walk and obedience He wants? What does He tell them to pursue? Is there any mention of pursuing God through any lesser way?

ONE STEP FURTHER:

But what of us?

If the wisest man ever to live finished badly, what hope do we have today? Think through this question broadly. Consider what Solomon neglected as well as what Christians have today that he didn't have. We'll get to this more in *Voices, New Testament*. For now, reason through this question biblically and record your thoughts below.

In verse 6, what is tied with not keeping God's commandments and statutes?

What "other gods" do people worship and serve today?

How are you doing at walking in God's way? How can you improve?

IGNORING THE CLEAR COMMANDS AND FINISHING POORLY

The wisest man ever other than Jesus to live ignored and rebelled against God's clear commands and finished badly. Let's look at Solomon's tragic finish.

OBSERVE the TEXT of SCRIPTURE

READ 1 Kings 11:11-13. **MARK** every reference to God *(God, Lord)*. Then **MARK** every reference to God's *commands* and *statutes*.

1 Kings 11:1-13

1 Now King Solomon loved many foreign women along with the daughter of Pharaoh: Moabite, Ammonite, Edomite, Sidonian, and Hittite women,

2 from the nations concerning which the LORD had said to the sons of Israel, "You shall not associate with them, nor shall they associate with you, for they will surely turn your heart away after their gods." Solomon held fast to these in love.

3 He had seven hundred wives, princesses, and three hundred concubines, and his wives turned his heart away.

4 For when Solomon was old, his wives turned his heart away after other gods; and his heart was not wholly devoted to the LORD his God, as the heart of David his father had been.

5 For Solomon went after Ashtoreth the goddess of the Sidonians and after Milcom the detestable idol of the Ammonites.

6 Solomon did what was evil in the sight of the LORD, and did not follow the LORD fully, as David his father had done.

7 Then Solomon built a high place for Chemosh the detestable idol of Moab, on the mountain which is east of Jerusalem, and for Molech the detestable idol of the sons of Ammon.

8 Thus also he did for all his foreign wives, who burned incense and sacrificed to their gods.

9 Now the LORD was angry with Solomon because his heart was turned away from the LORD, the God of Israel, who had appeared to him twice,

10 and had commanded him concerning this thing, that he should not go after other gods; but he did not observe what the LORD had commanded.

11 So the LORD said to Solomon, "Because you have done this, and you have not kept My covenant and My statutes, which I have commanded you, I will surely tear the kingdom from you, and will give it to your servant.

12 "Nevertheless I will not do it in your days for the sake of your father David, but I will tear it out of the hand of your son.

13 "However, I will not tear away all the kingdom, but I will give one tribe to your son for the sake of My servant David and for the sake of Jerusalem which I have chosen."

DISCUSS with your GROUP or PONDER on your own . . .

What clear command does Solomon violate? How does he rebel against this?

Week Five: **Hard Words from a Sovereign God**

What did God threaten against this kind of sin? Clear enough?

Describe Solomon in his old age. How had his heart changed?

If Solomon had obeyed God's Word as revealed in the Torah (Genesis–Deuteronomy), how could his end-of-life been different?

What final word does Solomon receive from the Lord in verses 11-13?

@THE END OF THE DAY . . .

Take some time to think through any lingering presuppositions you have about how God communicates with those He loves. How do your views stack up against what you've seen so far from God's Word? Is what you're studying confirming what you thought or are you having to adjust your thinking to His? Ask God to guide you as you think through these questions and measure your answers against the truth of His Word and then write anything you need to remember below. Remember what Paul says in his letter to Timothy: "All Scripture is inspired by God and profitable for teaching, for reproof, for correction, for training in righteousness; so that the man of God may be adequate, equipped for every good work." If any of your views need correcting, correct them according to His Word and rejoice that He is faithful to discipline us as sons and daughters.

VOICES
HEARING GOD
IN A WORLD OF
IMPOSTORS

Old Testament

128

WEEK SIX
From God to Prophet to King

*Yet the LORD warned Israel and Judah through all His prophets
and every seer, saying, "Turn from your evil ways and keep My
commandments, My statutes according to all the law which I
commanded your fathers, and which I sent to you through
My servants the prophets."
However, they did not listen, but stiffened their neck
like their fathers, who did not believe in the LORD their God.*

—2 Kings 17:13-14

Among believers who seek a fresh "word from God" it is common to want the word from God to be positive and affirming. Biblical history particularly during times of grave national sin, shows the opposite was most often true. During the monarchy in Israel and Judah, God communicated with the kings, typically through prophets. The words, though occasionally encouraging, were not characteristically "cheery." Rather, they were generally judgmental and threatening.

This week we'll survey God's words to the kings, as well as false voices that claimed to speak for God and consider how to guard ourselves against similar false voices today.

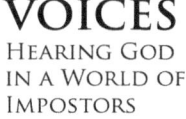

VOICES
HEARING GOD
IN A WORLD OF
IMPOSTORS

Old Testament

129

GOD ESTABLISHES JEROBOAM

After Solomon's disobedience, God tore ten of Israel's twelve tribes away from his son, Rehoboam, and gave them to a man named Jeroboam. From this point forward, the once United Kingdom of Israel became two separate entities: ten tribes now called "Israel" in the north and two tribes called "Judah" in the south. In order to keep the information a little more clear, we'll look at how God spoke to Israel first and then consider His dealings with Judah. Let's take a look

OBSERVE the TEXT of SCRIPTURE

READ 1 Kings 11:28-38. **MARK** every reference to the phrase *I will.*

1 Kings 11:28-38

28 *Now the man Jeroboam was a valiant warrior, and when Solomon saw that the young man was industrious, he appointed him over all the forced labor of the house of Joseph.*

29 *It came about at that time, when Jeroboam went out of Jerusalem, that the prophet Ahijah the Shilonite found him on the road. Now Ahijah had clothed himself with a new cloak; and both of them were alone in the field.*

30 *Then Ahijah took hold of the new cloak which was on him and tore it into twelve pieces.*

31 *He said to Jeroboam, "Take for yourself ten pieces; for thus says the LORD, the God of Israel, 'Behold, I will tear the kingdom out of the hand of Solomon and give you ten tribes*

32 *(but he will have one tribe, for the sake of My servant David and for the sake of Jerusalem, the city which I have chosen from all the tribes of Israel),*

33 *because they have forsaken Me, and have worshiped Ashtoreth the goddess of the Sidonians, Chemosh the god of Moab, and Milcom the god of the sons of Ammon; and they have not walked in My ways, doing what is right in My sight and observing My statutes and My ordinances, as his father David did.*

34 *'Nevertheless I will not take the whole kingdom out of his hand, but I will make him ruler all the days of his life, for the sake of My servant David whom I chose, who observed My commandments and My statutes;*

35 *but I will take the kingdom from his son's hand and give it to you, even ten tribes.*

36 *'But to his son I will give one tribe, that My servant David may have a lamp always before Me in Jerusalem, the city where I have chosen for Myself to put My name.*

37 *'I will take you, and you shall reign over whatever you desire, and you shall be king over Israel.*

38 *'Then it will be, that if you listen to all that I command you and walk in My ways, and do what is right in My sight by observing My statutes and My commandments, as My servant David did, then I will be with you and build you an enduring house as I built for David, and I will give Israel to you.*

ONE STEP FURTHER:

Who was Jeroboam?

If you have extra time, do a little research this week to see what you can learn about Jeroboam. Record your findings below.

DISCUSS with your GROUP or PONDER on your own . . .

Describe Jeroboam.

Describe Ahijah.

What message does God send to Jeroboam through Ahijah? What visual aid does he use?

What does God say He will do? (Make a list based on your markings.)

Why does God tear ten tribes away from Solomon? Had He been sufficiently clear with Solomon? Explain.

What does God expect from Jeroboam? Is He clear?

ONE STEP FURTHER:

Jeroboam Doubts God's Word

Jeroboam immediately doubts the word of the Lord he hears from the prophet. Check out 1 Kings 12:25-33 and record your observations below.

VOICES
HEARING GOD
IN A WORLD OF
IMPOSTORS

Old Testament   131

JEROBOAM DOUBTS GOD'S CLEAR WORD

If you've done your One Step Further options, you've seen that Jeroboam doubted the clear word of God and set out on his own path. God warned Jeroboam but he never repented. In this next text, we'll see God speak again but they are words that predict devastation for Jeroboam and his family.

OBSERVE the TEXT of SCRIPTURE

READ 1 Kings 14:1-20. **MARK** every reference to *Ahijah*, the prophet.

1 Kings 14:1-20

1 At that time Abijah the son of Jeroboam became sick.

2 Jeroboam said to his wife, "Arise now, and disguise yourself so that they will not know that you are the wife of Jeroboam, and go to Shiloh; behold, Ahijah the prophet is there, who spoke concerning me that I would be *king over this people.*

3 "Take ten loaves with you, some cakes and a jar of honey, and go to him. He will tell you what will happen to the boy."

4 Jeroboam's wife did so, and arose and went to Shiloh, and came to the house of Ahijah. Now Ahijah could not see, for his eyes were dim because of his age.

5 Now the LORD had said to Ahijah, "Behold, the wife of Jeroboam is coming to inquire of you concerning her son, for he is sick. You shall say thus and thus to her, for it will be when she arrives that she will pretend to be another woman."

6 When Ahijah heard the sound of her feet coming in the doorway, he said, "Come in, wife of Jeroboam, why do you pretend to be another woman? For I am sent to you with a harsh message.

7 "Go, say to Jeroboam, 'Thus says the LORD God of Israel, "Because I exalted you from among the people and made you leader over My people Israel,

8 and tore the kingdom away from the house of David and gave it to you—yet you have not been like My servant David, who kept My commandments and who followed Me with all his heart, to do only that which was right in My sight;

9 you also have done more evil than all who were before you, and have gone and made for yourself other gods and molten images to provoke Me to anger, and have cast Me behind your back—

10 therefore behold, I am bringing calamity on the house of Jeroboam, and will cut off from Jeroboam every male person, both bond and free in Israel, and I will make a clean sweep of the house of Jeroboam, as one sweeps away dung until it is all gone.

11 "Anyone belonging to Jeroboam who dies in the city the dogs will eat. And he who dies in the field the birds of the heavens will eat; for the LORD has spoken it." '

12 "Now you, arise, go to your house. When your feet enter the city the child will die.

ONE STEP FURTHER:

God Sends a Warning
In 1 Kings 13, God sends a harsh message to Jeroboam's kingdom. If you have time, check it out and record your findings below.

13 *"All Israel shall mourn for him and bury him, for he alone of Jeroboam's family will come to the grave, because in him something good was found toward the LORD God of Israel in the house of Jeroboam.*

14 *"Moreover, the LORD will raise up for Himself a king over Israel who will cut off the house of Jeroboam this day and from now on.*

15 *"For the LORD will strike Israel, as a reed is shaken in the water; and He will uproot Israel from this good land which He gave to their fathers, and will scatter them beyond the Euphrates River, because they have made their Asherim, provoking the LORD to anger.*

16 *"He will give up Israel on account of the sins of Jeroboam, which he committed and with which he made Israel to sin."*

17 *Then Jeroboam's wife arose and departed and came to Tirzah. As she was entering the threshold of the house, the child died.*

18 *All Israel buried him and mourned for him, according to the word of the LORD which He spoke through His servant Ahijah the prophet.*

19 *Now the rest of the acts of Jeroboam, how he made war and how he reigned, behold, they are written in the Book of the Chronicles of the Kings of Israel.*

20 *The time that Jeroboam reigned was twenty-two years; and he slept with his fathers, and Nadab his son reigned in his place.*

ONE STEP FURTHER:

Word Study: Harsh

If you have time this week, find the Hebrew word that translates "harsh." How else is it used throughout the Old Testament? Record your findings below.

DISCUSS with your GROUP or PONDER on your own . . .

When Jeroboam's son becomes sick, where does he send for information? What does he tell his wife to do? Does it help?

Describe Ahijah and his condition. What does the LORD tell him and when?

What kind of message does God send Jeroboam? Give specifics.

VOICES
HEARING GOD
IN A WORLD OF
IMPOSTORS

Week Six: **From God to Prophet to King**

What will happen to the child? Why? (Think carefully here and consider what is going to happen to the other descendants.)

Does the word of the prophet come true? When?

How has Jeroboam gotten himself into this fix?

What cautionary principles does his life provide for us?

ACCORDING TO THE WORD OF THE LORD

Jeroboam's son Abijah dies according to the word of the LORD in a merciful manner, the only one of his house in whom "something good was found toward the LORD." Another son, Nadab, ascends the throne only to be quickly overthrown by Baasha who kills him and reigns in his place. Baasha had received word from the LORD through the prophet Jehu, son of Hanani. Let's take a look at it.

OBSERVE the TEXT of SCRIPTURE

READ 1 Kings 16:1-4 and **MARK** every reference to *the LORD*.

1 Kings 16:1-4

1 Now the word of the LORD came to Jehu the son of Hanani against Baasha, saying,

2 "Inasmuch as I exalted you from the dust and made you leader over My people Israel, and you have walked in the way of Jeroboam and have made My people Israel sin, provoking Me to anger with their sins,

3 behold, I will consume Baasha and his house, and I will make your house like the house of Jeroboam the son of Nebat.

4 "Anyone of Baasha who dies in the city the dogs will eat, and anyone of his who dies in the field the birds of the heavens will eat."

FYI:

The End of the Story

Thus Zimri destroyed all the household of Baasha, according to the word of the LORD, which He spoke against Baasha through Jehu the prophet . . .
—1 Kings 16:12

DISCUSS with your GROUP or PONDER on your own . . .

How does the LORD send word to King Baasha?

What has Baasha done wrong? What will result?

Compare God's message to Jeroboam with His message to Baasha. How are they similar? How do they differ?

THE BADDEST OF THE BAD

All of Israel's kings were evil: Jeroboam, Nadab, Baasha, Elah, Zimri, and Omri. Omri's son Ahab proved more wicked than any Israelite king before or after him even though God continually warned him through the prophets. Let's look at a couple of instances when the LORD sent messages to him.

VOICES
HEARING GOD
IN A WORLD OF
IMPOSTORS

Old Testament

135

Week Six: **From God to Prophet to King**

OBSERVE the TEXT of SCRIPTURE

READ 1 Kings 20 in your Bible. Pay close attention to God's purposes and Ahab's behavior.

DISCUSS with your GROUP or PONDER on your own . . .

What is the context surrounding God's first message to Ahab? Was Ahab seeking the LORD for counsel? Explain.

Why does the LORD send him the message? What does the prophet tell Ahab to do? Does he listen? What happens?

What second message does God send through the prophet? How is it fulfilled?

What third message does God send? What will God do and why? How is it fulfilled?

What critical error does Ahab make after his win? What did he refuse to do that the LORD commanded him to do?

How does the LORD explain it in His fourth message to Ahab in this chapter? What does he tell Ahab in verse 42?

Do people today intermittently obey and disobey a single command from God? Do they obey some of God's commands and disobey others? How did this work for Ahab? How will it work for us?

Digging Deeper

Elijah and Elisha

If you have some extra time, look into the lives of Elijah and Elisha. What does God say to them in 1 and 2 Kings? Is the text clear on how He spoke? Who were the messages for? When and why did He speak? See what you can discover and record your observations below.

Elijah

Elisha

ONE STEP FURTHER:

Obeying the Word of the Lord to the Prophets
If you have some time this week, compare the judgment of the man in 1 Kings 20:35-36 with that of the young prophet in 1 Kings 13. Was it important for people to obey the revealed Word of God? Record your observations below.

FYI:

Hebrews
It is a terrifying thing to fall into the hands of the living God.
—Hebrews 10:31

VOICES
HEARING GOD
IN A WORLD OF
IMPOSTORS

Old Testament

AN UNSOUGHT WORD FROM GOD

Ahab's son, Ahaziah, doesn't seek the LORD's voice, but he ends up hearing from Him regardless. Let's take a look.

OBSERVE the TEXT of SCRIPTURE

READ 1 Kings 22:51–2 Kings 1:17 and **MARK** every reference to *Ahaziah*.

1 Kings 22:51–2 Kings 1:17

51 Ahaziah the son of Ahab became king over Israel in Samaria in the seventeenth year of Jehoshaphat king of Judah, and he reigned two years over Israel.

52 He did evil in the sight of the LORD and walked in the way of his father and in the way of his mother and in the way of Jeroboam the son of Nebat, who caused Israel to sin.

53 So he served Baal and worshiped him and provoked the LORD God of Israel to anger, according to all that his father had done.

1 Now Moab rebelled against Israel after the death of Ahab.

2 And Ahaziah fell through the lattice in his upper chamber which was in Samaria, and became ill. So he sent messengers and said to them, "Go, inquire of Baal-zebub, the god of Ekron, whether I will recover from this sickness."

3 But the angel of the LORD said to Elijah the Tishbite, "Arise, go up to meet the messengers of the king of Samaria and say to them, 'Is it because there is no God in Israel that you are going to inquire of Baal-zebub, the god of Ekron?'

4 "Now therefore thus says the LORD, 'You shall not come down from the bed where you have gone up, but you shall surely die.' " Then Elijah departed.

5 When the messengers returned to him he said to them, "Why have you returned?"

6 They said to him, "A man came up to meet us and said to us, 'Go, return to the king who sent you and say to him, "Thus says the LORD, 'Is it because there is no God in Israel that you are sending to inquire of Baal-zebub, the god of Ekron? Therefore you shall not come down from the bed where you have gone up, but shall surely die.' " ' "

7 He said to them, "What kind of man was he who came up to meet you and spoke these words to you?"

8 They answered him, "He was a hairy man with a leather girdle bound about his loins." And he said, "It is Elijah the Tishbite."

9 Then the king sent to him a captain of fifty with his fifty. And he went up to him, and behold, he was sitting on the top of the hill. And he said to him, "O man of God, the king says, 'Come down.' "

10 Elijah replied to the captain of fifty, "If I am a man of God, let fire come down from heaven and consume you and your fifty." Then fire came down from heaven and consumed him and his fifty.

ONE STEP FURTHER:

The Rest of the Story of Ahab

If you have time this week, check out other times God sent word to Ahab and how he responded. Don't miss 1 Kings 21:18-29 and the fulfillment in 1 Kings 22:38.

---

11 So he again sent to him another captain of fifty with his fifty. And he said to him, "O man of God, thus says the king, 'Come down quickly.' "

12 Elijah replied to them, "If I am a man of God, let fire come down from heaven and consume you and your fifty." Then the fire of God came down from heaven and consumed him and his fifty.

13 So he again sent the captain of a third fifty with his fifty. When the third captain of fifty went up, he came and bowed down on his knees before Elijah, and begged him and said to him, "O man of God, please let my life and the lives of these fifty servants of yours be precious in your sight.

14 "Behold fire came down from heaven and consumed the first two captains of fifty with their fifties; but now let my life be precious in your sight."

15 The angel of the LORD said to Elijah, "Go down with him; do not be afraid of him." So he arose and went down with him to the king.

16 Then he said to him, "Thus says the LORD, 'Because you have sent messengers to inquire of Baal-zebub, the god of Ekron—is it because there is no God in Israel to inquire of His word?—therefore you shall not come down from the bed where you have gone up, but shall surely die.' "

17 So Ahaziah died according to the word of the LORD which Elijah had spoken. And because he had no son, Jehoram became king in his place in the second year of Jehoram the son of Jehoshaphat, king of Judah.

> **FYI:**
>
> **Rejecting God's Voice**
> The sons of Israel walked in all the sins of Jeroboam which he did; they did not depart from them until the LORD removed Israel from His sight, as He spoke through all His servants the prophets. So Israel was carried away into exile from their own land to Assyria until this day.
> —2 Kings 17:22-23

DISCUSS with your GROUP or PONDER on your own . . .

Describe Ahaziah. Who was his father? Who, likely, was his mother? How did he take after his father's example?

Why is he seeking a medical prognosis? Who does he seek an answer from? What does this reveal about him?

Who sends him an answer instead? How does it come? What is the message?

VOICES
HEARING GOD
IN A WORLD OF
IMPOSTORS

Old Testament

How is it authenticated and repeated?

According to 2 Kings 1:17, what happens to Ahaziah?

If Ahaziah had been obeying God's Law would he have needed a word from God?

Does this account change your thinking about "a word of the LORD"? Explain.

ONE STEP FURTHER:

What are you doing here?

If you have some extra time this week, dig into 1 Kings 19. After Elijah's victory over the prophets of Baal and Jezebel's subsequent threat to kill him, Elijah flees to Mount Horeb (also called Sinai) where God had met with Moses. What did Elijah say to God? What questions and instructions did God have for Elijah? How did Elijah finish? What can we learn? Record your findings below.

GOD SENDS A WORD OF DESTRUCTION

After Ahaziah's death, God commissions Jehu to take out Ahaziah's brother, King Jehoram.

OBSERVE the TEXT of SCRIPTURE

READ 2 Kings 9:1-10 **MARK** every reference to *the LORD* and to *Jehu*, including pronouns.

2 Kings 9:1-10

1   *Now Elisha the prophet called one of the sons of the prophets and said to him, "Gird up your loins, and take this flask of oil in your hand and go to Ramoth-gilead.*

VOICES
HEARING GOD
IN A WORLD OF
IMPOSTORS

140

Old Testament

2 *"When you arrive there, search out Jehu the son of Jehoshaphat the son of Nimshi, and go in and bid him arise from among his brothers, and bring him to an inner room.*

3 *"Then take the flask of oil and pour it on his head and say, 'Thus says the LORD, "I have anointed you king over Israel." ' Then open the door and flee and do not wait."*

4 *So the young man, the servant of the prophet, went to Ramoth-gilead.*

5 *When he came, behold, the captains of the army were sitting, and he said, "I have a word for you, O captain." And Jehu said, "For which one of us?" And he said, "For you, O captain."*

6 *He arose and went into the house, and he poured the oil on his head and said to him, "Thus says the LORD, the God of Israel, 'I have anointed you king over the people of the LORD, even over Israel.*

7 *'You shall strike the house of Ahab your master, that I may avenge the blood of My servants the prophets, and the blood of all the servants of the LORD, at the hand of Jezebel.*

8 *'For the whole house of Ahab shall perish, and I will cut off from Ahab every male person both bond and free in Israel.*

9 *'I will make the house of Ahab like the house of Jeroboam the son of Nebat, and like the house of Baasha the son of Ahijah.*

10 *'The dogs shall eat Jezebel in the territory of Jezreel, and none shall bury her.' " Then he opened the door and fled.*

DISCUSS with your GROUP or PONDER on your own . . .

Who does God use to deliver His message to Jehu? What is the news for Jehu? What is the assignment? Why?

Is the message consistent with other messages from God? Explain. (See also 1 Kings 21:19.)

FYI:

A Deadly Legacy

As we survey the kings of the northern kingdom, it quickly becomes clear that they are all bad. Jehu has one shining moment of obedience and some kings rate higher on the wicked meter than others, but all of the kings of Israel follow the path of Jeroboam who rebelled against the clear word of God. Their deadly legacy is one of hardened hearts and stopped-up ears toward the Word of the LORD.

FYI:

Jehu's Reward

The LORD said to Jehu, "Because you have done well in executing what is right in My eyes, and have done to the house of Ahab according to all that was in My heart, your sons of the fourth generation shall sit on the throne of Israel."
—2 Kings 10:30

VOICES
HEARING GOD
IN A WORLD OF
IMPOSTORS

GOD SENDS WORD TO SOLOMON'S SON

At the division of the kingdom God gives Jeroboam the ten tribes and calls off Rehoboam when he wants to engage his rival in battle.

OBSERVE the TEXT of SCRIPTURE

READ 1 Kings 12:22-24 **MARK** every reference to *the LORD*.

1 Kings 12:22-24

22 *But the word of God came to Shemaiah the man of God, saying,*

23 *"Speak to Rehoboam the son of Solomon, king of Judah, and to all the house of Judah and Benjamin and to the rest of the people, saying,*

24 *'Thus says the LORD, "You must not go up and fight against your relatives the sons of Israel; return every man to his house, for this thing has come from Me." ' " So they listened to the word of the LORD, and returned and went their way according to the word of the LORD.*

DISCUSS with your GROUP or PONDER on your own . . .

How does God speak to Rehoboam?

What command does He give? How does He explain it?

How do Rehoboam and the people respond?

VOICES
HEARING GOD
IN A WORLD OF
IMPOSTORS

Old Testament

DAVID'S DESCENDANT INQUIRES OF GOD

Although Rehoboam *received* God's Word through a messenger, his great-grandson Jehoshaphat *sought* God's Word.

OBSERVE the TEXT of SCRIPTURE

READ 1 Kings 22 paying close attention to the difference between the true and false voices. Then, in the text below, **MARK** every reference to the prophets in Ahab's court.

1 Kings 22:5-28

5   Moreover, Jehoshaphat said to the king of Israel, "Please inquire first for the word of the LORD."

6   Then the king of Israel gathered the prophets together, about four hundred men, and said to them, "Shall I go against Ramoth-gilead to battle or shall I refrain?" And they said, "Go up, for the Lord will give it into the hand of the king."

7   But Jehoshaphat said, "Is there not yet a prophet of the LORD here that we may inquire of him?"

8   The king of Israel said to Jehoshaphat, "There is yet one man by whom we may inquire of the LORD, but I hate him, because he does not prophesy good concerning me, but evil. He is Micaiah son of Imlah." But Jehoshaphat said, "Let not the king say so."

9   Then the king of Israel called an officer and said, "Bring quickly Micaiah son of Imlah."

10 Now the king of Israel and Jehoshaphat king of Judah were sitting each on his throne, arrayed in their robes, at the threshing floor at the entrance of the gate of Samaria; and all the prophets were prophesying before them.

11 Then Zedekiah the son of Chenaanah made horns of iron for himself and said, "Thus says the LORD, 'With these you will gore the Arameans until they are consumed.' "

12 All the prophets were prophesying thus, saying, "Go up to Ramoth-gilead and prosper, for the LORD will give it into the hand of the king."

13 Then the messenger who went to summon Micaiah spoke to him saying, "Behold now, the words of the prophets are uniformly favorable to the king. Please let your word be like the word of one of them, and speak favorably."

14 But Micaiah said, "As the LORD lives, what the LORD says to me, that I shall speak."

15 When he came to the king, the king said to him, "Micaiah, shall we go to Ramoth-gilead to battle, or shall we refrain?" And he answered him, "Go up and succeed, and the LORD will give it into the hand of the king."

16 Then the king said to him, "How many times must I adjure you to speak to me nothing but the truth in the name of the LORD?"

ONE STEP FURTHER:

Jehoshaphat's Divided Heart

If you have extra time this week, examine the life of Jehoshaphat more closely. In what ways did he follow and listen to God? In what ways did he ignore God's voice and clear instruction? What can we learn from his entanglements with the sinful northern kingdom? Record your observations below.

VOICES
HEARING GOD
IN A WORLD OF
IMPOSTORS

Week Six: **From God to Prophet to King**

17 So he said,

"I saw all Israel

Scattered on the mountains,

Like sheep which have no shepherd.

And the LORD said, 'These have no master.

Let each of them return to his house in peace.' "

18 Then the king of Israel said to Jehoshaphat, "Did I not tell you that he would not prophesy good concerning me, but evil?"

19 Micaiah said, "Therefore, hear the word of the LORD. I saw the LORD sitting on His throne, and all the host of heaven standing by Him on His right and on His left.

20 "The LORD said, 'Who will entice Ahab to go up and fall at Ramoth-gilead?' And one said this while another said that.

21 "Then a spirit came forward and stood before the LORD and said, 'I will entice him.'

22 "The LORD said to him, 'How?' And he said, 'I will go out and be a deceiving spirit in the mouth of all his prophets.' Then He said, 'You are to entice him and also prevail. Go and do so.'

23 "Now therefore, behold, the LORD has put a deceiving spirit in the mouth of all these your prophets; and the LORD has proclaimed disaster against you."

24 Then Zedekiah the son of Chenaanah came near and struck Micaiah on the cheek and said, "How did the Spirit of the LORD pass from me to speak to you?"

25 Micaiah said, "Behold, you shall see on that day when you enter an inner room to hide yourself."

26 Then the king of Israel said, "Take Micaiah and return him to Amon the governor of the city and to Joash the king's son;

27 and say, 'Thus says the king, "Put this man in prison and feed him sparingly with bread and water until I return safely." ' "

28 Micaiah said, "If you indeed return safely the LORD has not spoken by me." And he said, "Listen, all you people."

DISCUSS with your GROUP or PONDER on your own . . .

Describe the political situation. Which nations are allies and which are enemies?

Who is "the king of Israel" at this time in history? (If you're not sure, check the end of 1 Kings 21.)

What does Jehoshaphat of Judah want the king of Israel to do prior to going to battle? How does the king of Israel respond? Why doesn't this satisfy Jehoshaphat?

Describe the prophets from Ahab's court. Make a simple list based on your markings. Don't miss recording *whose* prophets they are (v. 22). What is their message?

Who do they eventually call in? What does the king of Israel think about him?

How does the message of the 400 prophets differ from Micaiah's message?

How does Micaiah explain the difference?

Week Six: **From God to Prophet to King**

What is the fundamental difference between true and false prophets in this section? How long did it take to know the difference? Does this have any application today? Explain why or why not.

FYI:

Presumptuous Prophets
You may say in your heart, "How will we know the word which the LORD has not spoken?" When a prophet speaks in the name of the LORD, if the thing does not come about or come true, that is the thing which the LORD has not spoken. The prophet has spoken it presumptuously; you shall not be afraid of him.
—Deuteronomy 18:21-22

How does Micaiah say the king and the people will know if he has spoken truthfully and that the others have spoken falsehood? Consider Deuteronomy 18:21-22 as you answer.

Do false prophets still exist? What are ways we can recognize them?

THE WORD OF THE LORD WAS WITH ELISHA

Jehoshaphat of Judah has a similar experience later when he decides to go to war with Ahab's son, King Jehoram of Israel.

OBSERVE the TEXT of SCRIPTURE

READ 2 Kings 3. Then, in the text below, **MARK** every occurrence of *prophet(s)*.

2 Kings 3:11-19

11 But Jehoshaphat said, "Is there not a prophet of the Lord here, that we may inquire of the Lord by him?" And one of the king of Israel's servants answered and said, "Elisha the son of Shaphat is here, who used to pour water on the hands of Elijah."

12 Jehoshaphat said, "The word of the Lord is with him." So the king of Israel and Jehoshaphat and the king of Edom went down to him.

13 Now Elisha said to the king of Israel, "What do I have to do with you? Go to the prophets of your father and to the prophets of your mother." And the king of Israel said to him, "No, for the Lord has called these three kings together to give them into the hand of Moab."

14 Elisha said, "As the Lord of hosts lives, before whom I stand, were it not that I regard the presence of Jehoshaphat the king of Judah, I would not look at you nor see you.

15 "But now bring me a minstrel." And it came about, when the minstrel played, that the hand of the Lord came upon him.

16 He said, "Thus says the Lord, 'Make this valley full of trenches.'

17 "For thus says the Lord, 'You shall not see wind nor shall you see rain; yet that valley shall be filled with water, so that you shall drink, both you and your cattle and your beasts.

18 'This is but a slight thing in the sight of the Lord; He will also give the Moabites into your hand.

19 'Then you shall strike every fortified city and every choice city, and fell every good tree and stop all springs of water, and mar every good piece of land with stones.' "

DISCUSS with your GROUP or PONDER on your own . . .

What is the political situation? Which kings are allies? Who are they after and why?

What predicament do they find themselves in? What does Jehoshaphat propose to help them?

How is Elisha described?

How does Elisha respond to the King of Israel?

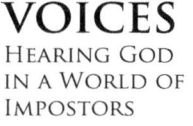

VOICES
HEARING GOD
IN A WORLD OF
IMPOSTORS

Week Six: **From God to Prophet to King**

What prophets does the text mention? What do we know about each? (As you answer, remember who Jehoram's dad was and who his mom probably was.)

What message do the kings get from God? How does He send it? How is it fulfilled?

What does the text show Elisha to be? How does he compare with the prophets of Jehoram's parents?

@THE END OF THE DAY . . .

Take some time to summarize what you've learned this week. Consider specifically the instances of false voices in the lives of the kings. Where did false voices lead them? If we listen to false voices today, where will they lead us?

WEEK SEVEN
More Words from God through the Prophets

Yet He sent prophets to them to bring them back to the LORD; though they testified against them, they would not listen.

—2 Chronicles 24:19

While God spoke directly to Solomon in a vision, during the time of the kings of Israel and Judah God repeatedly sent words through the prophets to kings usually because of their lack of adherence to His written commands.

This week, we'll look at an example of extreme disobedience and one of profound obedience among the kings of Judah. We'll also look at God's communication with another world leader, Nebuchadnezzar, during the time of Judah's captivity in Babylon and at the physical and emotional toll that God's revelation took on Daniel.

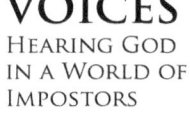

VOICES
HEARING GOD
IN A WORLD OF
IMPOSTORS

Old Testament

149

NOTES

MANASSEH REJECTS THE WORD OF THE LORD

While the kings of Israel all rebelled against God, the kings of Judah were a mixed bag of very good, very bad, and everything in between. Manasseh, though, was the worst king in the southern kingdom of Judah . . . by far. Surprisingly his father, Hezekiah, was good and his grandson, Josiah, was exceptionally good. Manasseh, however, was everything but.

ONE STEP FURTHER:

Hezekiah of Judah

If you have time this week, check out Hezekiah's story on your own. How did God speak to him? How did Hezekiah respond? Did he live well? How did he finish? You'll find his story in 2 Kings 18–21, 2 Chronicles 29–32, and Isaiah 36–39. Record your findings below.

OBSERVE the TEXT of SCRIPTURE

READ 2 Kings 21:1-15. **MARK** the phrase *did evil*. **UNDERLINE** phrases that describe the evil.

2 Kings 21:1-15

1   Manasseh was twelve years old when he became king, and he reigned fifty-five years in Jerusalem; and his mother's name was Hephzibah.

2   He did evil in the sight of the LORD, according to the abominations of the nations whom the LORD dispossessed before the sons of Israel.

3   For he rebuilt the high places which Hezekiah his father had destroyed; and he erected altars for Baal and made an Asherah, as Ahab king of Israel had done, and worshiped all the host of heaven and served them.

4   He built altars in the house of the LORD, of which the LORD had said, "In Jerusalem I will put My name."

5   For he built altars for all the host of heaven in the two courts of the house of the LORD.

6   He made his son pass through the fire, practiced witchcraft and used divination, and dealt with mediums and spiritists. He did much evil in the sight of the LORD provoking Him to anger.

7   Then he set the carved image of Asherah that he had made, in the house of which the LORD said to David and to his son Solomon, "In this house and in Jerusalem, which I have chosen from all the tribes of Israel, I will put My name forever.

8   "And I will not make the feet of Israel wander anymore from the land which I gave their fathers, if only they will observe to do according to all that I have commanded them, and according to all the law that My servant Moses commanded them."

9   But they did not listen, and Manasseh seduced them to do evil more than the nations whom the LORD destroyed before the sons of Israel.

10   Now the LORD spoke through His servants the prophets, saying,

11   "Because Manasseh king of Judah has done these abominations, having done wickedly more than all the Amorites did who were before him, and has also made Judah sin with his idols;

12   therefore thus says the LORD, the God of Israel, 'Behold, I am bringing such calamity on Jerusalem and Judah, that whoever hears of it, both his ears will tingle.

VOICES
HEARING GOD
IN A WORLD OF
IMPOSTORS

150

Old Testament

13 'I will stretch over Jerusalem the line of Samaria and the plummet of the house of Ahab, and I will wipe Jerusalem as one wipes a dish, wiping it and turning it upside down.

14 'I will abandon the remnant of My inheritance and deliver them into the hand of their enemies, and they will become as plunder and spoil to all their enemies;

15 because they have done evil in My sight, and have been provoking Me to anger since the day their fathers came from Egypt, even to this day.' "

DISCUSS with your GROUP or PONDER on your own . . .

Describe Manasseh. How old was he when he became king? How long did he rule? What characterizes his reign?

Had God warned against these kinds of actions? If so, where? What did He specifically command?

What did the LORD say to David and Solomon about the temple where Manasseh worshipped his idols? (vv. 7-8) What conditions did He attach?

Did the people obey Moses' words? How does the text describe their behavior in verse 9?

FYI:

"Passed through the Fire"
Leviticus 18:21 says, "You shall not give any of your offspring to offer them to Molech." While unthinkable in modern times, child sacrifice—causing children to "pass through the fire" as an offering to the idol, Molech—was practiced by some of the peoples Israel dispossessed of the land. Child sacrifice was one of numerous abominations Manasseh endorsed and committed.

FYI:

The Longest Reign
Manasseh's 55-year reign in Judah ranks as the longest in the history of God's chosen people among all the kings in the Northern, Southern, and United Kingdoms.

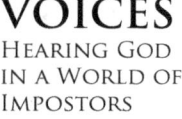

VOICES
HEARING GOD
IN A WORLD OF
IMPOSTORS

Based on Manasseh's disobedience, what does God say He will do? How does He send His message?

What effect does Manasseh's sin have on his people?

How have you noticed the reach of sin in your life and in culture today? Are your examples of faith and sin significant in others' lives? Explain.

OBSERVE the TEXT of SCRIPTURE

READ the parallel account of Manasseh from 2 Chronicles 33:1-13. This time **MARK** every reference to *Manasseh*, including pronouns.

2 Chronicles 33:1-13

1   *Manasseh was twelve years old when he became king, and he reigned fifty-five years in Jerusalem.*

2   *He did evil in the sight of the LORD according to the abominations of the nations whom the LORD dispossessed before the sons of Israel.*

3   *For he rebuilt the high places which Hezekiah his father had broken down; he also erected altars for the Baals and made Asherim, and worshiped all the host of heaven and served them.*

4   *He built altars in the house of the LORD of which the LORD had said, "My name shall be in Jerusalem forever."*

5   *For he built altars for all the host of heaven in the two courts of the house of the LORD.*

6   *He made his sons pass through the fire in the valley of Ben-hinnom; and he practiced witchcraft, used divination, practiced sorcery and dealt with mediums and spiritists. He did much evil in the sight of the LORD, provoking Him to anger.*

7   Then he put the carved image of the idol which he had made in the house of God, of which God had said to David and to Solomon his son, "In this house and in Jerusalem, which I have chosen from all the tribes of Israel, I will put My name forever;

8   and I will not again remove the foot of Israel from the land which I have appointed for your fathers, if only they will observe to do all that I have commanded them according to all the law, the statutes and the ordinances given *through Moses.*"

9   Thus Manasseh misled Judah and the inhabitants of Jerusalem to do more evil than the nations whom the LORD destroyed before the sons of Israel.

10 The LORD spoke to Manasseh and his people, but they paid no attention.

11 Therefore the LORD brought the commanders of the army of the king of Assyria against them, and they captured Manasseh with hooks, bound him with bronze chains *and took him to Babylon.*

12 When he was in distress, he entreated the LORD his God and humbled himself greatly before the God of his fathers.

13 When he prayed to Him, He was moved by his entreaty and heard his supplication, and brought him again to Jerusalem to his kingdom. Then Manasseh knew that the LORD was God.

DISCUSS with your GROUP or PONDER on your own . . .

What does Manasseh's leadership do to his people?

How do they compare with the nations God destroyed when bringing Israel into the land? Does God warn them? How do they respond?

What eventually happens to Manasseh?

VOICES
HEARING GOD
IN A WORLD OF
IMPOSTORS

Old Testament   153

Does God still warn today? If so, how? Explain your answer.

ONE STEP FURTHER:

Humbled and Repentant

If you have time this week, read the account of Manasseh's end-of-life repentance in 2 Chronicles 33:10–20. As you read, note what Manasseh finally "listened" to. Record your observations below.

How do people today ignore God? Do you ever ignore His warnings? Explain.

A YOUNG, LISTENING KING

Although Chronicles records Manasseh's end-of-life repentance after his stay at the Babylon Hilton, there was no undoing his years and years of evil and blood pollution in Judah. The destruction of his kingdom was inevitable, but not before an outstanding grandson ushered in a brief time of revival that was quite literally "by the Book."

OBSERVE the TEXT of SCRIPTURE

READ 2 Kings 22 and 2 Chronicles 34:1-7. **MARK** references to *the house of the LORD* and to *the book of the law.*

2 Kings 22

1 *Josiah was eight years old when he became king, and he reigned thirty-one years in Jerusalem; and his mother's name was Jedidah the daughter of Adaiah of Bozkath.*

2 *He did right in the sight of the LORD and walked in all the way of his father David, nor did he turn aside to the right or to the left.*

3 *Now in the eighteenth year of King Josiah, the king sent Shaphan, the son of Azaliah the son of Meshullam the scribe, to the house of the LORD saying,*

4 *"Go up to Hilkiah the high priest that he may count the money brought in to the house of the LORD which the doorkeepers have gathered from the people.*

5 *"Let them deliver it into the hand of the workmen who have the oversight of the house of the LORD, and let them give it to the workmen who are in the house of the LORD to repair the damages of the house,*

6 *to the carpenters and the builders and the masons and for buying timber and hewn stone to repair the house.*

7 *"Only no accounting shall be made with them for the money delivered into their hands, for they deal faithfully."*

8   Then Hilkiah the high priest said to Shaphan the scribe, "I have found the book of the law in the house of the LORD." And Hilkiah gave the book to Shaphan who read it.

9   Shaphan the scribe came to the king and brought back word to the king and said, "Your servants have emptied out the money that was found in the house, and have delivered it into the hand of the workmen who have the oversight of the house of the LORD."

10   Moreover, Shaphan the scribe told the king saying, "Hilkiah the priest has given me a book." And Shaphan read it in the presence of the king.

11   When the king heard the words of the book of the law, he tore his clothes.

12   Then the king commanded Hilkiah the priest, Ahikam the son of Shaphan, Achbor the son of Micaiah, Shaphan the scribe, and Asaiah the king's servant saying,

13   "Go, inquire of the LORD for me and the people and all Judah concerning the words of this book that has been found, for great is the wrath of the LORD that burns against us, because our fathers have not listened to the words of this book, to do according to all that is written concerning us."

14   So Hilkiah the priest, Ahikam, Achbor, Shaphan, and Asaiah went to Huldah the prophetess, the wife of Shallum the son of Tikvah, the son of Harhas, keeper of the wardrobe (now she lived in Jerusalem in the Second Quarter); and they spoke to her.

15   She said to them, "Thus says the LORD God of Israel, 'Tell the man who sent you to me,

16   thus says the LORD, "Behold, I bring evil on this place and on its inhabitants, even all the words of the book which the king of Judah has read.

17   "Because they have forsaken Me and have burned incense to other gods that they might provoke Me to anger with all the work of their hands, therefore My wrath burns against this place, and it shall not be quenched." '

18   "But to the king of Judah who sent you to inquire of the LORD thus shall you say to him, 'Thus says the LORD God of Israel, "Regarding the words which you have heard,

19   because your heart was tender and you humbled yourself before the LORD when you heard what I spoke against this place and against its inhabitants that they should become a desolation and a curse, and you have torn your clothes and wept before Me, I truly have heard you," declares the LORD.

20   "Therefore, behold, I will gather you to your fathers, and you will be gathered to your grave in peace, and your eyes will not see all the evil which I will bring on this place." ' " So they brought back word to the king.

2 Chronicles 34:1-7 (This gives us a little more info on Josiah's early years.)

1   Josiah was eight years old when he became king, and he reigned thirty-one years in Jerusalem.

2   He did right in the sight of the LORD, and walked in the ways of his father David and did not turn aside to the right or to the left.

> **FYI:**
>
> **Huldah the Prophetess**
> Though little is known about Huldah—in fact, nothing beyond the biblical text—we learn that she was a female among the true prophets of God. Moses' sister Miriam and Deborah, a judge, are two others Scripture identifies. It's interesting to note that while both Jeremiah and Zephaniah were Huldah's contemporaries, Josiah sends to her to inquire of God for him when the book of the Law is discovered in the temple.

3 For in the eighth year of his reign while he was still a youth, he began to seek the God of his father David; and in the twelfth year he began to purge Judah and Jerusalem of the high places, the Asherim, the carved images and the molten images.

4 They tore down the altars of the Baals in his presence, and the incense altars that were high above them he chopped down; also the Asherim, the carved images and the molten images he broke in pieces and ground to powder and scattered it on the graves of those who had sacrificed to them.

5 Then he burned the bones of the priests on their altars and purged Judah and Jerusalem.

6 In the cities of Manasseh, Ephraim, Simeon, even as far as Naphtali, in their surrounding ruins,

7 he also tore down the altars and beat the Asherim and the carved images into powder, and chopped down all the incense altars throughout the land of Israel. Then he returned to Jerusalem.

FYI:

Josiah Prophesied by Name

Josiah's act of burning the priests' bones on the altar was prophesied in 1 Kings 13:1–2 by the man of God who was sent to King Jeroboam. Not only was the action foretold but also Josiah was called by name: "Now behold, there came a man of God from Judah to Bethel by the word of the LORD, while Jeroboam was standing by the altar to burn incense. He cried against the altar by the word of the LORD, and said, "O altar, altar, thus says the LORD, 'Behold, a son shall be born to the house of David, Josiah by name; and on you he shall sacrifice the priests of the high places who burn incense on you, and human bones shall be burned on you.'"

DISCUSS with your GROUP or PONDER on your own . . .

Describe Josiah's early years. How does he compare with Grandpa Manasseh?

How does Josiah conduct himself prior to having God's written Word?

Second Chronicles 34:3 says that Josiah began to seek God in the eighth year of his reign. What does he do in the twelfth year of his reign?

What does Hilkiah find in Josiah's eighteenth year? Where does he find it?

VOICES
HEARING GOD
IN A WORLD OF
IMPOSTORS

156

Old Testament

Although Josiah was doing his best to follow God's ways including having the temple repaired, how does he respond when he hears the written word of God? Why?

Why does Josiah inquire of God through Huldah the prophetess?

What message does God send to Josiah through her?

OBSERVE the TEXT of SCRIPTURE

READ 2 Kings 23:1-3. **MARK** every occurrence of the word *all*.

2 Kings 23:1-3

1   Then the king sent, and they gathered to him all the elders of Judah and of Jerusalem.

2   The king went up to the house of the LORD and all the men of Judah and all the inhabitants of Jerusalem with him, and the priests and the prophets and all the people, both small and great; and he read in their hearing all the words of the book of the covenant which was found in the house of the LORD.

3   The king stood by the pillar and made a covenant before the LORD, to walk after the LORD, and to keep His commandments and His testimonies and His statutes with all his heart and all his soul, to carry out the words of this covenant that were written in this book. And all the people entered into the covenant.

ONE STEP FURTHER:

Josiah's Timeline
If you can, invest some time this week in writing out for yourself a timeline of Josiah's life that includes dates and key events in his life.

Age	Event

What key event sparked a true relationship with God? Explain what it was and how it changed the rest of his life.

VOICES
HEARING GOD
IN A WORLD OF
IMPOSTORS

DISCUSS with your GROUP or PONDER on your own . . .

Who does Josiah gather to himself? Who goes up to the house of the LORD with him?

How many people does he read the words of the covenant to? How much of the book does he read?

What covenant does he enter into? How broad is it? How are the people involved?

How does having the written Word of God impact Josiah's life? The lives of Josiah's people? How are our spiritual lives hindered when we "lose" the Word of God in the busyness of life?

Are you committed to God's Word like Josiah was? Why/why not? If something needs to change, what is it? What will you do about it?

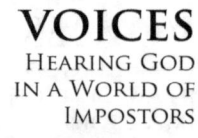

If you were fully committed to God's Word, what kind of a difference do you think it would make in your life?

JOSIAH SPARED CAPTIVITY

Although Josiah was certainly one of the best kings ever in Israel and Judah, in the end his failure to accept God's Word from an unlikely source resulted in his relatively early death. Yet, God sovereignly spared the good king from judgment at the hands of Babylon.

OBSERVE the TEXT of SCRIPTURE

READ 2 Chronicles 35:20-27. **MARK** references to *Josiah, Neco,* and *God.*

2 Chronicles 35:20-27

20 *After all this, when Josiah had set the temple in order, Neco king of Egypt came up to make war at Carchemish on the Euphrates, and Josiah went out to engage him.*

21 *But Neco sent messengers to him, saying, "What have we to do with each other, O King of Judah? I am not coming against you today but against the house with which I am at war, and God has ordered me to hurry. Stop for your own sake from interfering with God who is with me, so that He will not destroy you."*

22 *However, Josiah would not turn away from him, but disguised himself in order to make war with him; nor did he listen to the words of Neco from the mouth of God, but came to make war on the plain of Megiddo.*

23 *The archers shot King Josiah, and the king said to his servants, "Take me away, for I am badly wounded."*

24 *So his servants took him out of the chariot and carried him in the second chariot which he had, and brought him to Jerusalem where he died and was buried in the tombs of his fathers. All Judah and Jerusalem mourned for Josiah.*

25 *Then Jeremiah chanted a lament for Josiah. And all the male and female singers speak about Josiah in their lamentations to this day. And they made them an ordinance in Israel; behold, they are also written in the Lamentations.*

26 *Now the rest of the acts of Josiah and his deeds of devotion as written in the law of the LORD,*

27 *and his acts, first to last, behold, they are written in the Book of the Kings of Israel and Judah.*

FYI:

What We Don't Know
Just like Josiah, we can't live by God's Word if we don't know God's Word.

VOICES
HEARING GOD
IN A WORLD OF
IMPOSTORS

Old Testament   159

DISCUSS with your GROUP or PONDER on your own . . .

Who was Neco after? What message did he send to Josiah?

ONE STEP FURTHER:

Unlikely Mouthpieces

If you have time this week, record the unlikely messengers you've seen so far in this study. Pharaoh Neco is certainly one; who else comes to mind. List them below with references.

What does Josiah do? Does his strategy call to mind another king, one who was less than stellar?

Does Josiah inquire of God? What happens? Who laments him?

What are some qualities in Josiah's life that you'd like to be true of your life?

Digging Deeper

Modern "Visions of Heaven" and the Revealed Word

What do we make of the stories from people who claim to have been to heaven and back? "After death experiences" sell books and pique interest among many. How can we know truth about heaven? For starters, we can turn to the inspired accounts of Daniel, Ezekiel, and Isaiah in the Old Testament as well as to John, Stephen, and Paul in the New.

In each case, record what the prophet sees and hears. Then compare the accounts.

Daniel (Daniel 7:9-14)

Ezekiel (Ezekiel 1, 10)

Isaiah (Isaiah 6)

Summarize and compare the accounts.

If you have read any modern books that claim visions of heaven, how do they compare to the plumbline? (If you haven't read any of them, stick with the revealed word of God!)

GOD WORDS TO ANOTHER FOREIGN RULER

As God sent a dream to Pharaoh in Genesis, He sent one to another world ruler: Nebuchadnezzar of Babylon. After the northern kingdom of Israel continually rejected His words and warnings, God sent Assyria to judge the ten tribes. They conquered the nation by 722 BC, deported many of the citizens, and imported foreigners to live in the newly acquired land. The prophets had warned Israel of coming judgment if they did not keep God's covenant, but they neither listened nor obeyed.

Although Judah experienced a temporary revival of sorts under Josiah, she went the way of her wicked sister to the north. Having not only the warning of the prophets, but the example of God's judgment on Israel, Judah fell to the Babylonians. Nebuchadnezzar took most from Judah into captivity in Babylon and Jerusalem finally fell in 586 BC.

Unlike the scattering of Israel, Judah remained intact. Some people were left in the land and a remnant of those taken into captivity were eventually allowed to return.

During the time of Judah's captivity in Babylon, God communicated not only to his prophets Jeremiah (who remained in Judah until he was taken to Egypt), Ezekiel and Daniel (both taken to Babylon) but also to the Babylonian King Nebuchadnezzar. Let's take a look at Nebuchadnezzar's dream and the interpretation God sent through Daniel, a Jewish youth taken into captivity and trained for service to the king.

OBSERVE the TEXT of SCRIPTURE

READ Daniel 2. Then **MARK** every reference to *dream* and *interpretation.*

Daniel 2

1   *Now in the second year of the reign of Nebuchadnezzar, Nebuchadnezzar had dreams; and his spirit was troubled and his sleep left him.*

2   *Then the king gave orders to call in the magicians, the conjurers, the sorcerers and the Chaldeans to tell the king his dreams. So they came in and stood before the king.*

3   *The king said to them, "I had a dream and my spirit is anxious to understand the dream."*

4   *Then the Chaldeans spoke to the king in Aramaic: "O king, live forever! Tell the dream to your servants, and we will declare the interpretation."*

5   *The king replied to the Chaldeans, "The command from me is firm: if you do not make known to me the dream and its interpretation, you will be torn limb from limb and your houses will be made a rubbish heap.*

6   *"But if you declare the dream and its interpretation, you will receive from me gifts and a reward and great honor; therefore declare to me the dream and its interpretation."*

7   *They answered a second time and said, "Let the king tell the dream to his servants, and we will declare the interpretation."*

8   *The king replied, "I know for certain that you are bargaining for time, inasmuch as you have seen that the command from me is firm,*

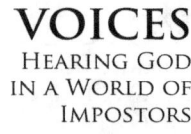

9 that if you do not make the dream known to me, there is only one decree for you. For you have agreed together to speak lying and corrupt words before me until the situation is changed; therefore tell me the dream, that I may know that you can declare to me its interpretation."

10 The Chaldeans answered the king and said, "There is not a man on earth who could declare the matter for the king, inasmuch as no great king or ruler has ever asked anything like this of any magician, conjurer or Chaldean.

11 "Moreover, the thing which the king demands is difficult, and there is no one else who could declare it to the king except gods, whose dwelling place is not with mortal flesh."

12 Because of this the king became indignant and very furious and gave orders to destroy all the wise men of Babylon.

13 So the decree went forth that the wise men should be slain; and they looked for Daniel and his friends to kill them.

14 Then Daniel replied with discretion and discernment to Arioch, the captain of the king's bodyguard, who had gone forth to slay the wise men of Babylon;

15 he said to Arioch, the king's commander, "For what reason is the decree from the king so urgent?" Then Arioch informed Daniel about the matter.

16 So Daniel went in and requested of the king that he would give him time, in order that he might declare the interpretation to the king.

17 Then Daniel went to his house and informed his friends, Hananiah, Mishael and Azariah, about the matter,

18 so that they might request compassion from the God of heaven concerning this mystery, so that Daniel and his friends would not be destroyed with the rest of the wise men of Babylon.

19 Then the mystery was revealed to Daniel in a night vision. Then Daniel blessed the God of heaven;

20 Daniel said,

"Let the name of God be blessed forever and ever,

For wisdom and power belong to Him.

21 "It is He who changes the times and the epochs;

He removes kings and establishes kings;

He gives wisdom to wise men

And knowledge to men of understanding.

22 "It is He who reveals the profound and hidden things;

He knows what is in the darkness,

And the light dwells with Him.

23 "To You, O God of my fathers, I give thanks and praise,

For You have given me wisdom and power;

Even now You have made known to me what we requested of You,

For You have made known to us the king's matter."

ONE STEP FURTHER:

Another Word to Nebuchadnezzar

Daniel interprets another dream from God for Nebuchadnezzar in chapter 4 that predicts a time of humbling for the king and advises him on how to prolong his prosperity. Within a year, though, the dream comes to pass and Nebuchadnezzar hears a voice from heaven. If you have time this week, check out Daniel 4 for yourself. Compare the dream with the fulfillment and see what Nebuchadnezzar learns for himself and what we can learn from his experience. Record your findings below.

24 Therefore, Daniel went in to Arioch, whom the king had appointed to destroy the wise men of Babylon; he went and spoke to him as follows: "Do not destroy the wise men of Babylon! Take me into the king's presence, and I will declare the interpretation to the king."

25 Then Arioch hurriedly brought Daniel into the king's presence and spoke to him as follows: "I have found a man among the exiles from Judah who can make the interpretation known to the king!"

26 The king said to Daniel, whose name was Belteshazzar, "Are you able to make known to me the dream which I have seen and its interpretation?"

27 Daniel answered before the king and said, "As for the mystery about which the king has inquired, neither wise men, conjurers, magicians nor diviners are able to declare it to the king.

28 "However, there is a God in heaven who reveals mysteries, and He has made known to King Nebuchadnezzar what will take place in the latter days. This was your dream and the visions in your mind while on your bed.

29 "As for you, O king, while on your bed your thoughts turned to what would take place in the future; and He who reveals mysteries has made known to you what will take place.

30 "But as for me, this mystery has not been revealed to me for any wisdom residing in me more than in any other living man, but for the purpose of making the interpretation known to the king, and that you may understand the thoughts of your mind.

Daniel declares and interprets the dream.

46 Then King Nebuchadnezzar fell on his face and did homage to Daniel, and gave orders to present to him an offering and fragrant incense.

47 The king answered Daniel and said, "Surely your God is a God of gods and a Lord of kings and a revealer of mysteries, since you have been able to reveal this mystery."

48 Then the king promoted Daniel and gave him many great gifts, and he made him ruler over the whole province of Babylon and chief prefect over all the wise men of Babylon.

49 And Daniel made request of the king, and he appointed Shadrach, Meshach and Abed-nego over the administration of the province of Babylon, while Daniel was at the king's court.

DISCUSS with your GROUP or PONDER on your own . . .

Briefly summarize Daniel 2.

What condition does Nebuchadnezzar's dream leave him in? What does he do as a result? What answers is he looking for?

How do his rules for interpretation keep potential liars at bay? What does this tell you about Nebuchadnezzar?

How do his own people, the Chaldeans, respond to his decree? What does this incite the king to order?

How do Daniel and his friends end up involved?

How does Daniel respond to the initial threat? What does he say and how does he say it? What does he ask Arioch for? What does he ask God for?

Why is Daniel able to answer the king's questions? What does he tell the king about his dream? What does he tell the king about his God?

ONE STEP FURTHER:

Handwriting on the Wall

Yup, this is where the phrase originates. God wrote on tablets at Sinai and caused a hand to write on a wall in Babylon. If you have time this week, dig into the account of God's message to King Belshazzar, King Nebuchadnezzar's descendant who based on history should have known better than to affront the God of Israel. As you read, note what the message was, how Daniel was involved in interpreting, and how quickly it came to pass. Record your findings below.

VOICES
HEARING GOD
IN A WORLD OF
IMPOSTORS

Old Testament   165

What was the dream? What did it mean? What did it reveal about Nebuchadnezzar? About God?

How does Nebuchadnezzar respond when Daniel declares the truth to him?

Why is it important to know that a voice or interpretation is true? How can we know?

How are you at responding to the clear Word of God that was once for all delivered to the saints (Jude 1:3)?

DANIEL'S VIEW OF SCRIPTURE

God's revelation to Daniel (which became Scripture) did not unhook him from prior written revelation. Rather, Daniel's life exemplifies knowing and living out the recorded Words of God. Daniel 9:4-15 particularly shows Daniel's pursuit of "the Law and the prophets" to understand Judah's current condition.

OBSERVE the TEXT of SCRIPTURE

READ Daniel 9:1-19 and **MARK** every reference to the revealed Word of God (*word, commandments, ordinances, voice,* etc.).

VOICES
HEARING GOD
IN A WORLD OF
IMPOSTORS

166

Old Testament

Daniel 9:1-19

1 In the first year of Darius the son of Ahasuerus, of Median descent, who was made king over the kingdom of the Chaldeans—

2 in the first year of his reign, I, Daniel, observed in the books the number of the years which was revealed as *the word of the Lord to Jeremiah the prophet for the completion of the desolations of Jerusalem,* namely, *seventy years.*

3 So I gave my attention to the Lord God to seek Him by *prayer and supplications, with fasting, sackcloth and ashes.*

4 I prayed to the Lord my God and confessed and said, "Alas, O Lord, the great and awesome God, who keeps His covenant and lovingkindness for those who love Him and keep His commandments,

5 we have sinned, committed iniquity, acted wickedly and rebelled, even turning aside from Your commandments and ordinances.

6 "Moreover, we have not listened to Your servants the prophets, who spoke in Your name to our kings, our princes, our fathers and all the people of the land.

7 "Righteousness belongs to You, O Lord, but to us open shame, as it is this day—to the men of Judah, the inhabitants of Jerusalem and all Israel, those who are nearby and those who are far away in all the countries to which You have driven them, because of their unfaithful deeds which they have committed against You.

8 "Open shame belongs to us, O Lord, to our kings, our princes and our fathers, because we have sinned against You.

9 "To the Lord our God belong compassion and forgiveness, for we have rebelled against Him;

10 nor have we obeyed the voice of the Lord our God, to walk in His teachings which He set before us through His servants the prophets.

11 "Indeed all Israel has transgressed Your law and turned aside, not obeying Your voice; so the curse has been poured out on us, along with the oath which is written in the law of Moses the servant of God, for we have sinned against Him.

12 "Thus He has confirmed His words which He had spoken against us and against our rulers who ruled us, to bring on us great calamity; for under the whole heaven there has not been done anything like what was done to Jerusalem.

13 "As it is written in the law of Moses, all this calamity has come on us; yet we have not sought the favor of the Lord our God by turning from our iniquity and giving attention to Your truth.

14 "Therefore the Lord has kept the calamity in store and brought it on us; for the Lord our God is righteous with respect to all His deeds which He has done, but we have not obeyed His voice.

15 "And now, O Lord our God, who have brought Your people out of the land of Egypt with a mighty hand and have made a name for Yourself, as it is this day—we have sinned, we have been wicked.

ONE STEP FURTHER:

Jeremiah 25

Take time this week to read Jeremiah's prophecy about the 70 years in captivity for yourself. Record what you learn below.

VOICES

HEARING GOD
IN A WORLD OF
IMPOSTORS

16 "O Lord, in accordance with all Your righteous acts, let now Your anger and Your wrath turn away from Your city Jerusalem, Your holy mountain; for because of our sins and the iniquities of our fathers, Jerusalem and Your people have become a reproach to all those around us.

17 "So now, our God, listen to the prayer of Your servant and to his supplications, and for Your sake, O Lord, let Your face shine on Your desolate sanctuary.

18 "O my God, incline Your ear and hear! Open Your eyes and see our desolations and the city which is called by Your name; for we are not presenting our supplications before You on account of any merits of our own, but on account of Your great compassion.

19 "O Lord, hear! O Lord, forgive! O Lord, listen and take action! For Your own sake, O my God, do not delay, because Your city and Your people are called by Your name."

DISCUSS with your GROUP or PONDER on your own . . .

Although Daniel saw visions from God, how does he know how long the captivity will last? What does he do when he learns God's plans?

What does Daniel confess? What have the people done with God's revelation?

What specifically did they do to bring a curse on themselves? How does Daniel know this? What plumbline is he measuring with?

ONE STEP FURTHER:

Compile a Bio on Daniel

Daniel is a biblical character beyond reproach. If you have some extra time this week, do a character study on him from the book of Daniel as well as from cross-references you can locate with a concordance. Then record your findings below.

VOICES
HEARING GOD
IN A WORLD OF
IMPOSTORS

168

Old Testament

How does Daniel define God's voice? (See vv. 10, 11, 14 and watch the context.)

Describe Daniel's view of God's Word. How does yours compare?

DANIEL'S RESPONSE TO VISIONS AND REVELATIONS

According to Hebrews 1:1, Old Testament prophets received God's revelation in "many portions and ways." "Portion" means no revelation was exhaustive and an example of a "way" is a vision accompanied by words.

We're not always told whether God communicated directly or indirectly in a vision or through an angel or prophet and this is the case with Daniel. We have been given, however, a first-hand look at the physical and emotional toll the messages Daniel received took on him.

While bookshelves today are filled with warm and fuzzy accounts of supposed messages from God, Daniel's experiences were everything but. It would be great for you to read the full accounts of the visions and revelations (if you have time, do it) but for our purposes now, let's focus on Daniel's response to the revelations.

OBSERVE the TEXT of SCRIPTURE

READ the following verses and **UNDERLINE** the effects the visions and revelations had on Daniel.

Daniel 7:15

15 *"As for me, Daniel, my spirit was distressed within me, and the visions in my mind kept alarming me."*

VOICES
HEARING GOD
IN A WORLD OF
IMPOSTORS

Week Seven: **More Words from God through the Prophets**

Daniel 7:28

28 "At this point the revelation ended. As for me, Daniel, my thoughts were greatly alarming me and my face grew pale, but I kept the matter to myself."

Daniel 8:15-17

15 When I, Daniel, had seen the vision, I sought to understand it; and behold, standing before me was one who looked like a man.

16 And I heard the voice of a man between the banks of *Ulai*, and he called out and said, "Gabriel, give this man an understanding of the vision."

17 So he came near to where I was standing, and when he came I was frightened and fell on my face; but he said to me, "Son of man, understand that the vision pertains to the time of the end."

Daniel 8:27

27 Then I, Daniel, was exhausted and sick for days. Then I got up again and carried on the king's business; but I was astounded at the vision, and there was none to explain it.

Daniel 10:4-12

4 On the twenty-fourth day of the first month, while I was by the bank of the great river, that is, the Tigris,

5 I lifted my eyes and looked, and behold, there was a certain man dressed in linen, whose waist was girded with a belt of *pure gold of Uphaz*.

6 His body also was like beryl, his face had the appearance of lightning, his eyes were like flaming torches, his arms and feet like the gleam of polished bronze, and the sound of his words like the sound of a tumult.

7 Now I, Daniel, alone saw the vision, while the men who were with me did not see the vision; nevertheless, a great dread fell on them, and they ran away to hide themselves.

8 So I was left alone and saw this great vision; yet no strength was left in me, for my natural color turned to a deathly pallor, and I retained no strength.

9 But I heard the sound of his words; and as soon as I heard the sound of his words, I fell into a deep sleep on my face, with my face to the ground.

10 Then behold, a hand touched me and set me trembling on my hands and knees.

11 He said to me, "O Daniel, man of high esteem, understand the words that I am about to tell you and stand upright, for I have now been sent to you." And when he had spoken this word to me, I stood up trembling.

12 Then he said to me, "Do not be afraid, Daniel, for from the first day that you set your heart on understanding this and on humbling yourself before your God, your words were heard, and I have come in response to your words."

Daniel 10:16-18

16 And behold, one who resembled a human being was touching my lips; then I opened my mouth and spoke and said to him who was standing before me, "O my lord, as a result of the vision anguish has come upon me, and I have retained no strength.

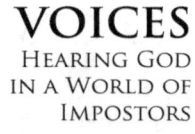

17 *"For how can such a servant of my lord talk with such as my lord? As for me, there remains just now no strength in me, nor has any breath been left in me."*

18 Then this *one with human appearance touched me again and strengthened me.*

DISCUSS with your GROUP or PONDER on your own . . .

Look back at what you've underlined and compile a simple list of the effects of the visions and revelations on Daniel.

How does this compare with what you've seen so far in the Old Testament? How did others respond to revelation? If you're familiar with John's account in Revelation, how does John's response to revelation (Revelation 1) compare with Daniel's?

Does this alter any pre-conceived ideas you've held? Explain.

How is God's revealed Word changing your thinking?

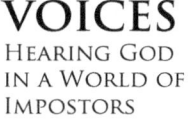

@THE END OF THE DAY . . .

Spend some time reviewing what you've studied this week. As you do, specifically consider how God's Word measures what we hear from other sources. Ask God to help you know His Word for yourself so you can discern and know the difference between His truth and clever lies.

WEEK EIGHT
On the Other Side of Judgment

Remember the word which You commanded Your servant Moses, say-
ing, "If you are unfaithful I will scatter you among the peoples; but if
you return to Me and keep My commandments and do them, though
those of you who have been scattered were in the most remote part
of the heavens, I will gather them from there and will bring them to the
place where I have chosen to cause My name to dwell."

—Nehemiah 1:8-9

God clearly laid out His covenant with His people and Moses recorded it for future generations. When they strayed, God sent His prophets to call the people back to the covenant. When they refused to heed the written Word and stopped up their ears to the prophets, God brought the judgments He warned them of. By 722 BC Assyria conquered and scattered the northern kingdom of Israel. Then in 586 BC Jerusalem, the capital of the southern kingdom, fell to Babylon. And, yet, God continued to lead His people. This week we'll focus most of our time on the days of Ezra and Nehemiah to see how God led them and stirred up the spirits of others to carry out His plan in His time.

VOICES
HEARING GOD
IN A WORLD OF
IMPOSTORS

Old Testament

173

GOD STIRS UP CYRUS

While God communicates in many ways throughout the Old Testament, the books of Ezra and Nehemiah in particular show another way He propels people. Let's take a look.

OBSERVE the TEXT of SCRIPTURE

READ Ezra 1:1-8 and **MARK** every reference to *Cyrus*, including pronouns.

Ezra 1:1-8

1 *Now in the first year of Cyrus king of Persia, in order to fulfill the word of the LORD by the mouth of Jeremiah, THE LORD STIRRED UP THE SPIRIT OF CYRUS KING OF PERSIA, so that he sent a proclamation throughout all his kingdom, and also* put it *in writing, saying:*

2 *"Thus says Cyrus king of Persia, 'The LORD, the God of heaven, has given me all the kingdoms of the earth and He has appointed me to build Him a house in Jerusalem, which is in Judah.*

3 *'Whoever there is among you of all His people, may his God be with him! Let him go up to Jerusalem which is in Judah and rebuild the house of the LORD, the God of Israel; He is the God who is in Jerusalem.*

4 *'Every survivor, at whatever place he may live, let the men of that place support him with silver and gold, with goods and cattle, together with a freewill offering for the house of God which is in Jerusalem.' "*

5 *Then the heads of fathers' households of Judah and Benjamin and the priests and the Levites arose, even everyone whose spirit God had stirred to go up and rebuild the house of the LORD which is in Jerusalem.*

6 *All those about them encouraged them with articles of silver, with gold, with goods, with cattle and with valuables, aside from all that was given as a freewill offering.*

7 *Also King Cyrus brought out the articles of the house of the LORD, which Nebuchadnezzar had carried away from Jerusalem and put in the house of his gods;*

8 *and Cyrus, king of Persia, had them brought out by the hand of Mithredath the treasurer, and he counted them out to Sheshbazzar, the prince of Judah.*

DISCUSS with your GROUP or PONDER on your own . . .

When and where do the events in Ezra 1 take place? Who's ruling? Where else is he mentioned in Scripture?

ONE STEP FURTHER:

Read Ezra

Try to make time this week to read the book of Ezra. It's only ten chapters long and we'll be reading the better part of two chapters in the lesson! Once you've read through it, record your observations below.

What does Cyrus do? Why does he do it?

How does God's work in Cyrus compare with His work in others before him?

The Word of the LORD in the Mouth of Jeremiah

It's amazing for a foreign king to send captives back to their homeland. It's even more amazing that exactly what happened was prophesied. Jeremiah 29:10 says "For thus says the Lord, 'When seventy years have been completed for Babylon, I will visit you and fulfill My good word to you, to bring you back to this place."

What does Jeremiah have to do with Cyrus's proclamation?

Beside Cyrus, who else does God stir up? What do they do?

What do others who are not stirred up do? How are they involved?

Does God stir up people today? Support your answer from Scripture.

VOICES
HEARING GOD
IN A WORLD OF
IMPOSTORS

Old Testament

GOD MOVES ARTAXERXES

After the temple is built, God works on another king—this time King Artaxerxes.

OBSERVE the TEXT of SCRIPTURE

READ Ezra 7 and MARK every reference to *Ezra* including pronouns. Then MARK references to the *law* including synonyms.

Ezra 7

1 Now after these things, in the reign of Artaxerxes king of Persia, there went up *Ezra son of Seraiah, son of Azariah, son of Hilkiah,*

2 *son of Shallum, son of Zadok, son of Ahitub,*

3 *son of Amariah, son of Azariah, son of Meraioth,*

4 *son of Zerahiah, son of Uzzi, son of Bukki,*

5 *son of Abishua, son of Phinehas, son of Eleazar, son of Aaron the chief priest.*

6 *This Ezra went up from Babylon, and he was a scribe skilled in the law of Moses, which the LORD God of Israel had given; and the king granted him all he requested because the hand of the LORD his God was upon him.*

7 *Some of the sons of Israel and some of the priests, the Levites, the singers, the gatekeepers and the temple servants went up to Jerusalem in the seventh year of King Artaxerxes.*

8 *He came to Jerusalem in the fifth month, which was in the seventh year of the king.*

9 *For on the first of the first month he began to go up from Babylon; and on the first of the fifth month he came to Jerusalem, because the good hand of his God was upon him.*

10 *For Ezra had set his heart to study the law of the LORD and to practice it, and to teach His statutes and ordinances in Israel.*

11 *Now this is the copy of the decree which King Artaxerxes gave to Ezra the priest, the scribe, learned in the words of the commandments of the LORD and His statutes to Israel:*

12 *"Artaxerxes, king of kings, to Ezra the priest, the scribe of the law of the God of heaven, perfect peace. And now*

13 *I have issued a decree that any of the people of Israel and their priests and the Levites in my kingdom who are willing to go to Jerusalem, may go with you.*

14 *"Forasmuch as you are sent by the king and his seven counselors to inquire concerning Judah and Jerusalem according to the law of your God which is in your hand,*

15 *and to bring the silver and gold, which the king and his counselors have freely offered to the God of Israel, whose dwelling is in Jerusalem,*

16 *with all the silver and gold which you find in the whole province of Babylon, along with the freewill offering of the people and of the priests, who offered willingly for the house of their God which is in Jerusalem;*

VOICES
HEARING GOD
IN A WORLD OF
IMPOSTORS

176

Old Testament

17 with this money, therefore, you shall diligently buy bulls, rams and lambs, with their grain offerings and their drink offerings and offer them on the altar of the house of your God which is in Jerusalem.

18 "Whatever seems good to you and to your brothers to do with the rest of the silver and gold, you may do according to the will of your God.

19 "Also the utensils which are given to you for the service of the house of your God, deliver in full before the God of Jerusalem.

20 "The rest of the needs for the house of your God, for which you may have occasion to provide, provide for it from the royal treasury.

21 "I, even I, King Artaxerxes, issue a decree to all the treasurers who are in the provinces beyond the River, that whatever Ezra the priest, the scribe of the law of the God of heaven, may require of you, it shall be done diligently,

22 even up to 100 talents of silver, 100 kors of wheat, 100 baths of wine, 100 baths of oil, and salt as needed.

23 "Whatever is commanded by the God of heaven, let it be done with zeal for the house of the God of heaven, so that there will not be wrath against the kingdom of the king and his sons.

24 "We also inform you that it is not allowed to impose tax, tribute or toll on any of the priests, Levites, singers, doorkeepers, Nethinim or servants of this house of God.

25 "You, Ezra, according to the wisdom of your God which is in your hand, appoint magistrates and judges that they may judge all the people who are in the province beyond the River, even all those who know the laws of your God; and you may teach anyone who is ignorant of them.

26 "Whoever will not observe the law of your God and the law of the king, let judgment be executed upon him strictly, whether for death or for banishment or for confiscation of goods or for imprisonment."

27 Blessed be the LORD, the God of our fathers, who has put such a thing as this in the king's heart, to adorn the house of the LORD which is in Jerusalem,

28 and has extended lovingkindness to me before the king and his counselors and before all the king's mighty princes. Thus I was strengthened according to the hand of the LORD my God upon me, and I gathered leading men from Israel to go up with me.

DISCUSS with your GROUP or PONDER on your own . . .

When and where do these events happen?

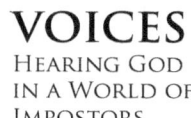

VOICES
HEARING GOD
IN A WORLD OF
IMPOSTORS

Old Testament

Week Eight: **On the Other Side of Judgment**

Briefly describe Ezra. Specifically address his attitude toward God's law.

Why does the king give Ezra what he requests?

What does Artaxerxes decree? What does he say directly to Ezra?

What does Ezra say about the king's decree in verse 27? What does the LORD have to do with the king's and Ezra's actions?

What benefits would people today get if they set their hearts on studying, practicing, and teaching God's Word? What benefits have you received?

GOD'S LEADING ON THE OTHER SIDE OF JUDGMENT

As the book of Nehemiah opens, Nehemiah is serving a foreign king in a foreign land in the years following God's judgment on Israel and Judah. Although God judged His people, He did not abandon them.

OBSERVE the TEXT of SCRIPTURE

READ Nehemiah 1:1-11. **MARK** every reference to *God's Word* (*commandments, statutes, ordinances, etc.*), to *sin,* and to *prayer*.

Nehemiah 1:1-11

1 The words of Nehemiah the son of Hacaliah.

Now it happened in the month Chislev, in the twentieth year, while I was in Susa the capitol,

2 that Hanani, one of my brothers, and some men from Judah came; and I asked them concerning the Jews who had escaped and had survived the captivity, and about Jerusalem.

3 They said to me, "The remnant there in the province who survived the captivity are in great distress and reproach, and the wall of Jerusalem is broken down and its gates are burned with fire."

4 When I heard these words, I sat down and wept and mourned for days; and I was fasting and praying before the God of heaven.

5 I said, "I beseech You, O LORD God of heaven, the great and awesome God, who preserves the covenant and lovingkindness for those who love Him and keep His commandments,

6 let Your ear now be attentive and Your eyes open to hear the prayer of Your servant which I am praying before You now, day and night, on behalf of the sons of Israel Your servants, confessing the sins of the sons of Israel which we have sinned against You; I and my father's house have sinned.

7 "We have acted very corruptly against You and have not kept the commandments, nor the statutes, nor the ordinances which You commanded Your servant Moses.

8 "Remember the word which You commanded Your servant Moses, saying, 'If you are unfaithful I will scatter you among the peoples;

9 but if you return to Me and keep My commandments and do them, though those of you who have been scattered were in the most remote part of the heavens, I will gather them from there and will bring them to the place where I have chosen to cause My name to dwell.'

10 "They are Your servants and Your people whom You redeemed by Your great power and by Your strong hand.

11 "O Lord, I beseech You, may Your ear be attentive to the prayer of Your servant and the prayer of Your servants who delight to revere Your name, and make Your servant successful today and grant him compassion before this man."

Now I was the cupbearer to the king.

ONE STEP FURTHER:

Read Nehemiah

While we'll look specifically at sections of the text relating to Nehemiah discerning God's will, it would be great for you to clear some time and read Nehemiah from front to back. Time invested in God's Word is *never* wasted! As you read, record your general observations below.

DISCUSS with your GROUP or PONDER on your own . . .

Where is Nehemiah as the book opens? Why is he there?

VOICES
HEARING GOD
IN A WORLD OF
IMPOSTORS

What prompts Nehemiah's weeping and mourning? What does he do as he weeps and mourns?

What does he ask God for? On what basis?

What does he confess? How does he know what to confess?

What does he know and claim from God's Word?

What is his final request to God in this section?

GOD SILENTLY OPENS A DOOR

After praying for compassion from the king and for success, Nehemiah goes about his business and God opens a door. King Artaxerxes asks Nehemiah the reason for his sad face. Nehemiah prays and answers. God grants him favor before the king who allows him to return to Judah to rebuild the wall around Jerusalem. Nehemiah realizes that this has happened because "the good hand of my God was on me" (2:8). We pick up the text with Nehemiah in Jerusalem.

OBSERVE the TEXT of SCRIPTURE

READ Nehemiah 2:11-18. **MARK** every reference to *Nehemiah*, including pronouns.

Nehemiah 2:11-18

11 *So I came to Jerusalem and was there three days.*

12 *And I arose in the night, I and a few men with me. I did not tell anyone what my God was putting into my mind to do for Jerusalem and there was no animal with me except the animal on which I was riding.*

13 *So I went out at night by the Valley Gate in the direction of the Dragon's Well and on to the Refuse Gate, inspecting the walls of Jerusalem which were broken down and its gates which were consumed by fire.*

14 *Then I passed on to the Fountain Gate and the King's Pool, but there was no place for my mount to pass.*

15 *So I went up at night by the ravine and inspected the wall. Then I entered the Valley Gate again and returned.*

16 *The officials did not know where I had gone or what I had done; nor had I as yet told the Jews, the priests, the nobles, the officials or the rest who did the work.*

17 *Then I said to them, "You see the bad situation we are in, that Jerusalem is desolate and its gates burned by fire. Come, let us rebuild the wall of Jerusalem so that we will no longer be a reproach."*

18 *I told them how the hand of my God had been favorable to me and also about the king's words which he had spoken to me. Then they said, "Let us arise and build." So they put their hands to the good work.*

> **FYI:**
>
> **"Putting Into My Mind"**
> The ESV translates Nehemiah 2:12: "Then I arose in the night, I and a few men with me. And I told no one what my God had ***put into my heart*** to do for Jerusalem" (bold italics mine).
> The NASB translates the Hebrew *leb* (literally "heart") as "mind." The OT's "heart" is most often the thinking faculty and here it is clear that God impressed an idea in Nehemiah's mind apart from any prophet bringing him a message.
> It's also important to watch how Nehemiah responds to this. He obeys what God is prompting him to do.

DISCUSS with your GROUP or PONDER on your own . . .

How does Nehemiah know what to do? How has God already been paving the way for him according to chapter 1?

What first steps does he take? What does he base his call to action to the people on?

Week Eight: **On the Other Side of Judgment**

How do the people respond?

When people today say "God told me to do this or that" what immediate questions does this bring up? What can we learn from Nehemiah?

DEMORALIZING VOICES RISE

Nehemiah 3 recounts in detail the building and repair of Jerusalem's wall. The men follow through on what God put in Nehemiah's mind/heart to do. In chapter 4, though, other voices start speaking.

OBSERVE the TEXT of SCRIPTURE

READ Nehemiah 4:1-5 and **UNDERLINE** what other "voices" say to the builders.

Nehemiah 4:1-5

1   *Now it came about that when Sanballat heard that we were rebuilding the wall, he became furious and very angry and mocked the Jews.*

2   *He spoke in the presence of his brothers and the wealthy men of Samaria and said, "What are these feeble Jews doing? Are they going to restore it for themselves? Can they offer sacrifices? Can they finish in a day? Can they revive the stones from the dusty rubble even the burned ones?"*

3   *Now Tobiah the Ammonite was near him and he said, "Even what they are building—if a fox should jump on it, he would break their stone wall down!"*

4   *Hear, O our God, how we are despised! Return their reproach on their own heads and give them up for plunder in a land of captivity.*

5   *Do not forgive their iniquity and let not their sin be blotted out before You, for they have demoralized the builders.*

DISCUSS with your GROUP or PONDER on your own . . .

Who is Sanballat (see 2:19) and how does he react to the Jews? What does he say?

Who is Tobiah and what does he say?

How does Nehemiah respond? How does he characterize what they have done to the builders?

Have you seen modern "Sanballats and Tobiahs" doing their work?

When you encounter these types, how do you typically respond? What can you learn from Nehemiah's handling of his enemies that can help you in dealing with demoralizers today?

Digging Deeper

False Prophets and Happy Talk

While Sanballat and Tobiah tried to discourage God's people with false words, lies don't always come packaged as discouragement. Some of the most potent dangers to God's people come from false prophets who proclaim happy words—words God has not put in their mouths—in perilous times. Try to make time this week to read and wrestle with the account of Hananiah and Jeremiah in Jeremiah 27–28.

Events in Jeremiah 27–28 take place in the beginning of the reign of King Zedekiah of Judah. The texts we have been reading in Daniel and Nehemiah show Jeremiah's prophecy of Jerusalem's "desolation" fulfilled.

What message does God give to Jeremiah regarding Nebuchadnezzar of Babylon? What visual aid accompanies the message? What warning does God send regarding prophets and others who give contrary messages?

Briefly describe Hananiah and summarize his prophecy. What does he predict? When will it come to pass? Did the message please the people?

The text refers to Hananiah and Jeremiah as prophets. How will the people know which prophet is speaking truth with respect to the duration of the captivity? Generally how can people know if a prophet is truly sent from the LORD?

What does Hananiah say regarding Jeremiah's prophecy? Who does he attribute the words to? What word does the Lord send back through Jeremiah? What happens to Hananiah? When?

Who was the true prophet?

VOICES
HEARING GOD
IN A WORLD OF
IMPOSTORS

184

Old Testament

REMEMBER THE LORD

The voices have an effect on the builders—they demoralized them. Still, in spite of both verbal opposition and the threat of physical violence the men of Judah continue to build. They pray and set up a guard.

OBSERVE the TEXT of SCRIPTURE

READ Nehemiah 4:14–21 and **MARK** references to *the work* including synonyms (*rebuilding*) and to various *weapons* (*sword, spear*, etc.).

Nehemiah 4:14–21

14 *When I saw their fear, I rose and spoke to the nobles, the officials and the rest of the people: "Do not be afraid of them; remember the Lord who is great and awesome, and fight for your brothers, your sons, your daughters, your wives and your houses."*

15 *When our enemies heard that it was known to us, and that God had frustrated their plan, then all of us returned to the wall, each one to his work.*

16 *From that day on, half of my servants carried on the work while half of them held the spears, the shields, the bows and the breastplates; and the captains were behind the whole house of Judah.*

17 *Those who were rebuilding the wall and those who carried burdens took their load with one hand doing the work and the other holding a weapon.*

18 *As for the builders, each wore his sword girded at his side as he built, while the trumpeter stood near me.*

19 *I said to the nobles, the officials and the rest of the people, "The work is great and extensive, and we are separated on the wall far from one another.*

20 *"At whatever place you hear the sound of the trumpet, rally to us there. Our God will fight for us."*

21 *So we carried on the work with half of them holding spears from dawn until the stars appeared.*

DISCUSS with your GROUP or PONDER on your own . . .

What does Nehemiah tell the people to do instead of being afraid? How does his instruction compare with those of leaders from other times in Israel's history?

ONE STEP FURTHER:

Word Study: Remember
When Nehemiah sees the Jews' fear, he tells them to "remember the Lord." If you have time this week, find the Hebrew word translated "remember" and see where it is used in the Old Testament. Who remembers? Who is told to remember? What are people told to remember and why? Ask some questions of your own, too, and record your findings below.

VOICES
HEARING GOD
IN A WORLD OF
IMPOSTORS

Old Testament

How do the people respond? What do they do? What war-time precautions do they take?

What assurance does Nehemiah give the people in verse 20?

When you find yourself in frightening situations, how does remembering the LORD help you?

SILENCING FALSE VOICES

In chapter 5, Nehemiah addresses the Jews' taking advantage of one another through such things as usury. He has proven to be an example of a servant leader who has not domineered the people. In chapter 6 that follows, he continues to stand against false accusations and lying voices, but this time they come in the form of "prophecies." Let's take a look.

OBSERVE the TEXT of SCRIPTURE

READ Nehemiah 6:1-16 and **MARK** every reference to *prophets* or *prophecy*.

Nehemiah 6:1-16

1   Now when it was reported to Sanballat, Tobiah, to Geshem the Arab and to the rest of our enemies that I had rebuilt the wall, and that *no breach remained in it,* although at that time I had not set up the doors in the gates,

2   then Sanballat and Geshem sent a message to me, saying, "Come, let us meet together at Chephirim in the plain of Ono." But they were planning to harm me.

3   So I sent messengers to them, saying, "I am doing a great work and I cannot come down. Why should the work stop while I leave it and come down to you?"

4   They sent messages *to me four times in this manner, and I answered them in the same way.*

5   *Then Sanballat sent his servant to me in the same manner a fifth time with an open letter in his hand.*

6   *In it was written,* "It is reported among the nations, and Gashmu says, that you and the Jews are planning to rebel; therefore you are rebuilding the wall. And you are to be their king, according to these reports.*

7   "You have also appointed prophets to proclaim in Jerusalem concerning you, 'A king is in Judah!' And now it will be reported to the king according to these reports. So come now, let us take counsel together.*"

8   *Then I sent* a message *to him saying,* "Such things as you are saying have not been done, but you are inventing them in your own mind.*"

9   *For all of them were trying to frighten us, thinking,* "They will become discouraged with the work and it will not be done.*" But now, O God, strengthen my hands.*

10   *When I entered the house of Shemaiah the son of Delaiah, son of Mehetabel, who was confined at home, he said,* "Let us meet together in the house of God, within the temple, and let us close the doors of the temple, for they are coming to kill you, and they are coming to kill you at night.*"

11   *But I said,* "Should a man like me flee? And could one such as I go into the temple to save his life? I will not go in.*"

12   *Then I perceived that surely God had not sent him, but he uttered* his *prophecy against me because Tobiah and Sanballat had hired him.*

13   *He was hired for this reason, that I might become frightened and act accordingly and sin, so that they might have an evil report in order that they could reproach me.*

14   *Remember, O my God, Tobiah and Sanballat according to these works of theirs, and also Noadiah the prophetess and the rest of the prophets who were* trying *to frighten me.*

15   *So the wall was completed on the twenty-fifth of* the month *Elul, in fifty-two days.*

16   *When all our enemies heard of it, and all the nations surrounding us saw* it, *they lost their confidence; for they recognized that this work had been accomplished with the help of our God.*

ONE STEP FURTHER:

Word Study: Perceive
Surrounded by lying voices, Nehemiah perceives the truth about Shemaiah. If you have some extra time this week, find the Hebrew word that translated "perceive." See where it is used in the Old Testament. How else is it translated? What does it involve? Finally, what do your word study tools have to say? Record your findings below.

DISCUSS with your GROUP or PONDER on your own . . .

What news do Nehemiah's enemies receive as the chapter opens?

VOICES
HEARING GOD
IN A WORLD OF
IMPOSTORS

Old Testament   187

Week Eight: **On the Other Side of Judgment**

What first message do Sanballat and Geshem send? Does Nehemiah "obey" their voice? Why/why not? Are they persistent or do they give up? Explain.

FYI:

Prophets for Profit
Her leaders pronounce judgment for a bribe,
Her priests instruct for a price
And her prophets divine for money.
Yet they lean on the LORD saying,
"Is not the LORD in our midst?
Calamity will not come upon us."
Therefore, on account of you
Zion will be plowed as a field,
Jerusalem will become a heap of ruins,
And the mountain of the temple will
become high places of a forest.
　　　　　　　　—Micah 3:11-12

How does the message change in Sanballat's fifth correspondence? What accusation does he make? How does Nehemiah respond to the false charges?

According to verse 9, what are the messages intended to do?

In verse 10, what prophecy does Shemaiah speak and why? What does Nehemiah "perceive" about him? How does Nehemiah perceive this? (Look closely at vv. 11-13 as you answer.)

Was Shemaiah the only one who prophesied for hire? Who else did and why?

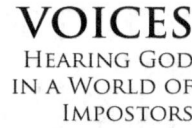

Do you think people prophesy today for hire? If so, how can you identify them? Explain your reasoning from Scripture.

Why is Nehemiah able to stand against these contrary voices?

If you had been in Nehemiah's place, would you have gone down from the wall in response to the first message? To any of the subsequent messages? Why/why not? How do you respond to similarly discouraging or threatening voices in your life?

What prime tool were the wrong voices using? What emotion were they trying to provoke in Nehemiah and the people?

What happens to Nehemiah's enemies when they hear of the wall's completion?

Week Eight: **On the Other Side of Judgment**

OBSERVE the TEXT of SCRIPTURE

READ Nehemiah 7:4-5 and **MARK** every reference to Nehemiah including pronouns.

Nehemiah 7:4-5

> 4 *Now the city was large and spacious, but the people in it were few and the houses were not built.*
>
> 5 *Then my God put it into my heart to assemble the nobles, the officials and the people to be enrolled by genealogies. Then I found the book of the genealogy of those who came up first in which I found the following record:*

DISCUSS with your GROUP or PONDER on your own . . .

Describe the city and its conditions.

How does Nehemiah describe the reason for his assembling and enrolling the people? How does this compare with what we have seen so far with regard to God's work in Nehemiah's life?

OBSERVE the TEXT of SCRIPTURE

READ Nehemiah 8:1-12 **MARK** *book* and/or *book of the law.*

Nehemiah 8:1-12

> 1 *And all the people gathered as one man at the square which was in front of the Water Gate, and they asked Ezra the scribe to bring the book of the law of Moses which the LORD had given to Israel.*
>
> 2 *Then Ezra the priest brought the law before the assembly of men, women and all who could listen with understanding, on the first day of the seventh month.*
>
> 3 *He read from it before the square which was in front of the Water Gate from early morning until midday, in the presence of men and women, those who could understand; and all the people were attentive to the book of the law.*

4   Ezra the scribe stood at a wooden podium which they had made for the purpose. And beside him stood Mattithiah, Shema, Anaiah, Uriah, Hilkiah, and Maaseiah on his right hand; and Pedaiah, Mishael, Malchijah, Hashum, Hashbaddanah, Zechariah and Meshullam on his left hand.

5   Ezra opened the book in the sight of all the people for he was standing above all the people; and when he opened it, all the people stood up.

6   Then Ezra blessed the LORD the great God. And all the people answered, "Amen, Amen!" while lifting up their hands; then they bowed low and worshiped the LORD with their faces to the ground.

7   Also Jeshua, Bani, Sherebiah, Jamin, Akkub, Shabbethai, Hodiah, Maaseiah, Kelita, Azariah, Jozabad, Hanan, Pelaiah, the Levites, explained the law to the people while the people remained in their place.

8   They read from the book, from the law of God, translating to give the sense so that they understood the reading.

9   Then Nehemiah, who was the governor, and Ezra the priest and scribe, and the Levites who taught the people said to all the people, "This day is holy to the LORD your God; do not mourn or weep." For all the people were weeping when they heard the words of the law.

10 Then he said to them, "Go, eat of the fat, drink of the sweet, and send portions to him who has nothing prepared; for this day is holy to our Lord. Do not be grieved, for the joy of the LORD is your strength."

11 So the Levites calmed all the people, saying, "Be still, for the day is holy; do not be grieved."

12 All the people went away to eat, to drink, to send portions and to celebrate a great festival, because they understood the words which had been made known to them.

DISCUSS with your GROUP or PONDER on your own . . .

How does God speak to the people in Nehemiah 8?

Who asks Ezra to bring the book of the law?

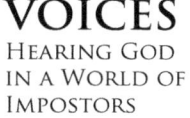

Week Eight: **On the Other Side of Judgment**

What does Ezra the scribe do with the book of the law? Who is involved and how long does it take?

How do the people respond? (Watch throughout the passage.)

What role do the Levites play in verses 8-9?

What is the result?

What can we learn from this for today? How is the Word of God important? Do you think people today need help in understanding it? If so, what kind?

VOICES
HEARING GOD
IN A WORLD OF
IMPOSTORS
Old Testament
192

"IS NOT MY WORD LIKE FIRE?"

As we close our time together, let's consider one final passage from the book of Jeremiah that looks not only at the problem of bad shepherds and false prophets in Jeremiah's time, but also at God's salvation which is to come!

OBSERVE the TEXT of SCRIPTURE

READ Jeremiah 23 and **MARK** every reference to God's Word in the text below. Then mark every reference to *prophets*.

Jeremiah 23

1 "Woe to the shepherds who are destroying and scattering the sheep of My pasture!" declares the LORD.

2 Therefore thus says the LORD God of Israel concerning the shepherds who are tending My people: "You have scattered My flock and driven them away, and have not attended to them; behold, I am about to attend to you for the evil of your deeds," declares the LORD.

3 "Then I Myself will gather the remnant of My flock out of all the countries where I have driven them and bring them back to their pasture, and they will be fruitful and multiply.

4 "I will also raise up shepherds over them and they will tend them; and they will not be afraid any longer, nor be terrified, nor will any be missing," declares the LORD.

5 "Behold, the days are coming," declares the LORD,

"When I will raise up for David a righteous Branch;

And He will reign as king and act wisely

And do justice and righteousness in the land.

6 "In His days Judah will be saved,

And Israel will dwell securely;

And this is His name by which He will be called,

'The LORD our righteousness.'

7 "Therefore behold, the days are coming," declares the LORD, "when they will no longer say, 'As the LORD lives, who brought up the sons of Israel from the land of Egypt,'

8 but, 'As the LORD lives, who brought up and led back the descendants of the household of Israel from the north land and from all the countries where I had driven them.' Then they will live on their own soil."

9 As for the prophets:

My heart is broken within me,

All my bones tremble;

I have become like a drunken man,

Even like a man overcome with wine,

VOICES
HEARING GOD
IN A WORLD OF
IMPOSTORS

Old Testament

193

Because of the LORD

And because of His holy words.

10 *For the land is full of adulterers;*

For the land mourns because of the curse.

The pastures of the wilderness have dried up.

Their course also is evil

And their might is not right.

11 *"For both prophet and priest are polluted;*

Even in My house I have found their wickedness," declares the LORD.

12 *"Therefore their way will be like slippery paths to them,*

They will be driven away into the gloom and fall down in it;

For I will bring calamity upon them,

The year of their punishment," declares the LORD.

13 *"Moreover, among the prophets of Samaria I saw an offensive thing:*

They prophesied by Baal and led My people Israel astray.

14 *"Also among the prophets of Jerusalem I have seen a horrible thing:*

The committing of adultery and walking in falsehood;

And they strengthen the hands of evildoers,

So that no one has turned back from his wickedness.

All of them have become to Me like Sodom,

And her inhabitants like Gomorrah.

15 *"Therefore thus says the LORD of hosts concerning the prophets,*

'Behold, I am going to feed them wormwood

And make them drink poisonous water,

For from the prophets of Jerusalem

Pollution has gone forth into all the land.' "

16 *Thus says the LORD of hosts,*

"Do not listen to the words of the prophets who are prophesying to you.

They are leading you into futility;

They speak a vision of their own imagination,

Not from the mouth of the LORD.

17 *"They keep saying to those who despise Me,*

'The LORD has said, "You will have peace" ';

And as for everyone who walks in the stubbornness of his own heart,

They say, 'Calamity will not come upon you.'

18 *"But who has stood in the council of the LORD,*

That he should see and hear His word?

Who has given heed to His word and listened?

19 *"Behold, the storm of the LORD has gone forth in wrath,*

Even a whirling tempest;

It will swirl down on the head of the wicked.

20 *"The anger of the LORD will not turn back*

Until He has performed and carried out the purposes of His heart;

In the last days you will clearly understand it.

21 *"I did not send these prophets,*

But they ran.

I did not speak to them,

But they prophesied.

22 *"But if they had stood in My council,*

Then they would have announced My words to My people,

And would have turned them back from their evil way

And from the evil of their deeds.

23 *"Am I a God who is near," declares the LORD,*

"And not a God far off?

24 *"Can a man hide himself in hiding places*

So I do not see him?" declares the LORD.

"Do I not fill the heavens and the earth?" declares the LORD.

25 *"I have heard what the prophets have said who prophesy falsely in My name, saying, 'I had a dream, I had a dream!'*

26 *"How long? Is there anything in the hearts of the prophets who prophesy falsehood, even these prophets of the deception of their own heart,*

27 *who intend to make My people forget My name by their dreams which they relate to one another, just as their fathers forgot My name because of Baal?*

28 *"The prophet who has a dream may relate his dream, but let him who has My word speak My word in truth. What does straw have in common with grain?" declares the LORD.*

29 *"Is not My word like fire?" declares the LORD, "and like a hammer which shatters a rock?*

30 *"Therefore behold, I am against the prophets," declares the LORD, "who steal My words from each other.*

31 *"Behold, I am against the prophets," declares the LORD, "who use their tongues and declare, 'The Lord declares.'*

32 *"Behold, I am against those who have prophesied false dreams," declares the LORD, "and related them and led My people astray by their falsehoods and reckless boasting; yet I did not send them or command them, nor do they furnish this people the slightest benefit," declares the LORD.*

VOICES
HEARING GOD
IN A WORLD OF
IMPOSTORS

Old Testament

Week Eight: **On the Other Side of Judgment**

33   *"Now when this people or the prophet or a priest asks you saying, 'What is the oracle of the LORD?' then you shall say to them, 'What oracle?' The LORD declares, 'I will abandon you.'*

34   *"Then as for the prophet or the priest or the people who say, 'The oracle of the LORD,' I will bring punishment upon that man and his household.*

35   *"Thus will each of you say to his neighbor and to his brother, 'What has the LORD answered?' or, 'What has the LORD spoken?'*

36   *"For you will no longer remember the oracle of the LORD, because every man's own word will become the oracle, and you have perverted the words of the living God, the LORD of hosts, our God.*

37   *"Thus you will say to that prophet, 'What has the LORD answered you?' and, 'What has the LORD spoken?'*

38   *"For if you say, 'The oracle of the LORD!' surely thus says the LORD, 'Because you said this word, "The oracle of the LORD!" I have also sent to you, saying, "You shall not say, 'The oracle of the LORD!' " '*

39   *"Therefore behold, I will surely forget you and cast you away from My presence, along with the city which I gave you and your fathers.*

40   *"I will put an everlasting reproach on you and an everlasting humiliation which will not be forgotten."*

DISCUSS with your GROUP or PONDER on your own . . .

Briefly summarize Jeremiah 23.

Questions based on verses 1–8

What does God say about His peoples' shepherds? What have they done? What will He do to them in return?

What future plans does the LORD have for "His flock"? What will the new shepherds be like?

Questions based on verses 9–17

What does the LORD say about the prophets and priests?

Could the people in Jeremiah's time blindly trust those in positions of spiritual authority without putting themselves in danger? Can we? Explain.

According to verse 16, what was the source of the prophecies?

Have you heard people today declare "Peace!" to those who walk in the stubbornness of their own hearts? How does this declaration compare with the clear teaching of Scripture?

Questions based on verses 18–29

How could the prophets have known God's truth? How can we?

What did the false prophets say according to verse 25? What do they prophesy according to verse 26?

ONE STEP FURTHER:

Word Study: Council
Jeremiah uses the word "council" (Hebrew: *sod*) twice in chapter 23. Take some time this week to study this word. See where it is used and how else it is translated. Can we stand in God's council today? If so, how? Record your findings below.

Week Eight: **On the Other Side of Judgment**

What are the prophets' dreams and God's Word compared to?

What point are these comparisons making?

Questions based on verses 30–40

What do the false prophets do and say? What is God's posture toward them?

Have you encountered any of these behaviors in person or in writing?

According to the text, what happens when people pervert the words of the living God?

How are you remembering and holding fast the Words of the living God today?

@THE END OF THE DAY . . .

As we bring this study to a close, go back and prayerfully consider what you have studied over the past eight weeks. What is the most significant truth you learned from God's Word? How is this truth changing how you think and act? Write it down below and ask God to etch it permanently on your heart.

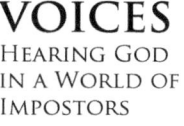

VOICES
HEARING GOD
IN A WORLD OF
IMPOSTORS

RESOURCES

Helpful Study Tools

The New How to Study Your Bible
Eugene, Oregon: Harvest House
Publishers

The New Inductive Study Bible
Eugene, Oregon: Harvest House
Publishers

Logos Bible Software
Available at www.logos.com.

Greek Word Study Tools

Kittel, G., Friedrich, G., & Bromiley,
G.W.
*Theological Dictionary of the New
Testament, Abridged* (also known as
Little Kittel)
Grand Rapids, Michigan: W.B.
Eerdmans Publishing Company

Zodhiates, Spiros
*The Complete Word Study Dictionary:
New Testament*
Chattanooga, Tennessee: AMG
Publishers

Hebrew Word Study Tools

Harris, R.L., Archer, G.L., & Walker,
B.K.
*Theological Wordbook of the Old
Testament* (also known as TWOT)
Chicago, Illinois: Moody Press

Zodhiates, Spiros
*The Complete Word Study Dictionary:
Old Testament*
Chattanooga, Tennessee: AMG
Publishers

General Word Study Tools

Strong, James
*The New Strong's Exhaustive
Concordance of the Bible*
Nashville, Tennessee: Thomas Nelson

Recommended Commentary Sets

Expositor's Bible Commentary
Grand Rapids, Michigan: Zondervan

NIV Application Commentary
Grand Rapids, Michigan: Zondervan

The New American Commentary
Nashville, Tennessee: Broadman and
Holman Publishers

One-Volume Commentary

Carson, D.A., France, R.T., Motyer,
J.A., & Wenham, G.J. Ed.
*New Bible Commentary: 21st Century
Edition*
Downers Grove, Illinois: Inter-Varsity
Press

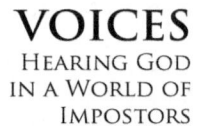

HOW TO DO AN ONLINE WORD STUDY

For use with www.blueletterbible.org

1. Type in Bible verse. Change the version to NASB. Click the "Search" button.
2. When you arrive at the next screen, click the "TOOLS" button to the left of your verse. This will open the blue "Interlinear" tab.
3. Click on the Strong's number which is the link to the original word in Greek or Hebrew.

Clicking this number will bring up another screen that will give you a brief definition of the word as well as list every occurrence of the Greek word in the New Testament or Hebrew word in the Old Testament. Before running to the dictionary definition, scan places where this word is used in Scripture and examine the general contexts where it is used.

VOICES
HEARING GOD
IN A WORLD OF
IMPOSTORS

Old Testament

We'd Love to Hear From You!

If you found this study helpful please take

a moment to share your thoughts.

Leave a Review

https://www.pamgillaspieshop.com/products/voices-old-testament

OR

Take a Short Survey

https://bit.ly/VoicesOTBookSurvey

www.ingramcontent.com/pod-product-compliance
Lightning Source LLC
Chambersburg PA
CBHW081657120626

46550CB00010B/2930